THE FOUNDATIONS OF MASTERY

With Love, Light &
Gratitude
Narina xxx

Dragonfly

Emerging from its watery bed, a winged perceiver
Gliding through the air, effortlessly
Masterful in flight
Hovering ethereally
Changing direction, swiftly
With inspiring lightness
Dazzling colours reflecting the light proudly, creatively
Ever flexible; highly adaptable
Fully present; highly attuned
Dragonfly, you have mastered water, air and light, in radiant colour
You have mastered movement and change, freedom and flow
A master of self, a powerful teacher
As you show us just how
You realise your fullest potential.

THE FOUNDATIONS OF MASTERY

12 STEPS TO A FULFILLED LIFE

BY
NARINA RISKOWITZ

This book is dedicated to you, the light bringers, light bearers, lightworkers of the world. Through your mastery the light is being anchored in on Earth, and the whole is uplifted and enlightened. Immense gratitude goes to you, great shining lights.

First published in Great Britain by Practical Inspiration
Publishing, 2019

ISBN 978-1-78860-035-4

Practical Inspiration
PUBLISHING

Table of Contents

List of Figures

List of Tables

Introduction

Self-Development to Self-Mastery

Life is a continuous process of self-discovery, evolution and growth. Like me, and many I've been working with, you may have been on the path of personal and spiritual development for a while now. Essentially, it's a healing journey – releasing fears, overcoming limiting beliefs, uncovering and integrating the unconscious shadow self, and coming into wholeness. Along the path of enlightenment, you may have had many 'aha' moments, moments of new insights and understanding. You may also have experienced moments of confusion; when you felt you knew nothing at all. Moments when you came across a new insight that blew your entire model of the world and you felt you had a blank slate again. Such moments can be confusing, yet they are signs of transformation. Confusion often precedes the next level of clarity and understanding. You may have had moments when you don't even know who you are. Either way, you've come a long way on your path of learning, discovery and growth. You may well feel ready for a whole new step or phase – to take a quantum leap to your next level of evolution. That may well be why you are holding this book in your hand. You are ready for self-mastery; mastering your energy, emotions, mind, thoughts, intuition, higher consciousness, and the art of manifesting health, happiness and fulfilment in your life.

Mastery? You may be thinking, 'Who am I to be a master?'

Who Do You Think You Are?

That's what I asked myself. Who do you think you are to write about mastery? You may be wondering too, who I am to write about mastery.

I've been working with individuals and groups as a Transformation Therapist and Soul Coach for many years now. I've been teaching Neurolinguistic Programming, Hypnosis, Meditation, Reiki, Healing and Spiritual Development courses for quite some time. I have seen people grow and advance greatly on their paths. There was a clear need for the next step. Self-mastery came as an inspiration. It felt big and important. It coincided with this significant time in our existence on Earth – a time of a radical shift in our own evolution.

When I embarked on this process of writing about mastery and facilitated the first courses on mastery, it felt daunting. It felt like a quantum leap and I soon realised, to take on a big concept, it will be essential to keep it simple. So, on this journey we are exploring the big concept of mastery, and we are going to keep it very simple and very practical. That's the good news!

If you're not thinking of yourself as a master yet, who do you think you are?

Laying the Foundation for Mastery

You are a Master so Discover your Greatness

You are a master, you've always been one. You came into this world a descending master. You carry mastery in your DNA. Inside of you is immense power, potential, gifts and abilities to be a leader, a change agent, a transformer, a beacon of light in a world that's been waiting for you. You have inner wisdom, waiting to be tapped, gifts and abilities ready to be unleashed. You are here with a great mission – to bring change to the world, to usher in a new way of being. You're not alone. You have a family of masters around you, ready to assist you in your task as a carrier of the light. The time is NOW – to step into your true power, own it and use it. The world needs the likes of you, NOW more than ever. Too often we under-estimate and doubt ourselves. It's time to step up. It's time to discover your greatness, step into it, be it, embrace it. It's time to uncover yourself as the ascending master. You are on the return journey, back home, back to your Self. The aim of this book is to assist you in that process. Not to make you a master, but to assist you in uncovering who you truly are and what you are capable of, and how you can be your true Masterful Self.

Of course you are ready for Mastery and if you're not sure yet, start by working through my first book: *Lifting the Veils of Illusion, 7 Steps to Spiritual Enlightenment* – this is likely to be the only preparation you may need.

Mastery is remembering who you are

Egoless, not Haughty

In discovering your greatness and your inherent power, how are you going to keep the ego out of it? We all know the ego loves the idea of power. So what kind of power are we talking about? Uncovering and stepping into your power is a key theme of mastery, one we will explore in-depth in Step 1 and Step 3. Here as we lay the foundation, let's recognise the ego and its tricks, give it a big reassuring hug that all will be well when we act from one whole integrated higher mind. Instead of fighting the ego, rather observe it, correct it and then lovingly integrate it into wholeness. True power is not haughty or arrogant or forceful. It's not perfection either. Nobody is perfect. It's not about the importance of the small self. It's about evolution into your greater self. Paradoxically, as your Higher Self, you are already perfect.

Lightness, not Serious

As we step up into mastery, it feels big. Let's not take ourselves too seriously. Truly spiritual people are refreshingly light-hearted.

Look at the Dalai Lama. When asked a question, he always laughs a hearty laugh, and then answers very simplistically. Ego can get very serious. Spirit is light-hearted (light in the heart).

Be the Master of Your Universe and Enjoy It!

Instead of wrestling the system or battling the perceived issues in the external world, continue to do the inner work of self-mastery. As you make changes in yourself, change is reflected externally as if by magic. The inside creates the outside. That's the mastery way of making change in the external world.

The Greatest of all Mastery Practices

Meditation

There are many reasons for maintaining a meditative practice. Taking time out to still your mind is essential for your health. During meditation you practise energy work to nourish, cleanse and re-energise yourself. Meditation is your time to go within and tune into your intuitive inner guidance. You can clear yourself of your day, let go, cut cords and practise forgiveness. During meditation you connect with your Higher Self and set your intentions. Meditation is your time of creation, restoration, healing, creation, connection and inner-tuition.

Forgiveness

If there was only one mastery practice, it would be forgiveness. The practice of forgiveness uncreates negative thought forms. Forgiveness clears perceptions of the past and heals tense relationships. Forgiveness is healing and creates a clean slate from where you can recreate your universe and all your relationships afresh. Miraculous work can be done with the forgiveness practice of *Ho'oponopono* discussed in Steps 4 and 9.

Responsibility

Mastery is taking responsibility for everything happening in your universe. You are the creator of your universe and taking full responsibility is immensely empowering. Anything playing out in your universe that's not quite according to plan can then be a great source of introspection. When you've gained the insights, you can exercise new choices and create afresh, assuring the outcomes you desire.

Discipline

Accomplished athletes, musicians and artists achieve mastery of their skills through the regular discipline of practice and action. Be equally disciplined about your mental energy and meditative practices. Over time, a regular practice of meditation will still the mind and alter your DNA and your universe in a way that is hugely rewarding.

Creating

You are essentially a creator and create all the time. As you deepen into mastery, you'll discover your immense creative potential and you will want to create your world consciously through intention and visualisation. Alberto Villoldo describes how the Laika, Inka, Hopi and Mayans knew that, when they inherited the created world, creation wasn't finished and that they were supposed to continue the creation process. The elders of these tribes meditate together, envisioning the world they want their grandchildren to inherit. The sages of old called this 'dreaming the world into being' (Villoldo, 2005 and 2007). You have the same power, so continue to co-create the world you desire. Continue to create light, good health, peace and joy in the world. Do so through thought-intention, visualisation and by being the light in the world.

Universal Spiritual Laws

Essential to mastery is a solid understanding and application of the Universal Spiritual Laws. The Laws governing the universe are as natural as the natural laws we are familiar with, such as the Law of Gravity. They are built into the fabric of the universe, reflecting the primary intelligence of the universe and are the guiding principles upon which the whole universe operates. They keep the universe and everything within it, in perfect order. Of course, on Earth we have free will in how we apply these principles – for selfish gain or for the betterment of the world – or whether we apply them at all. Yet, when we understand the Universal Spiritual Laws, they can guide us on our path and dramatically speed up our evolution and ascension. It is through the understanding and application of these laws that we can achieve mastery of our lives. These Spiritual Laws form part of the esoteric wisdom teaching of ancient Egypt, Israel, Greece, India, China and the like. Yet, the knowledge of it has somehow stopped being passed down and kept secret. If people knew they are in complete control of their minds and therefore their destiny, they would no longer be controlled by the governing, monetary and media systems of the world. Fortunately, modern quantum physics has also been proving these ancient principles to be accurate. Quantum physics allows for the quantum field of energy; the nothingness from where reality is constructed. This correlates perfectly with the ancient Buddhist concept that all reality is created by Mind from the Void. In a quantum universe, energy and consciousness are inseparable (Chopra, 2003). Conscious focus generates the energy that impacts particles and creates something out of nothing. Reality is a construct of the mind. Through the application of these spiritual and natural laws, you can master your own life and create your own destiny.

The 12 Chakra System

You may be familiar with the seven major chakras or energy centres of the human body, namely the Base, the Sacral, the Solar Plexus, the Heart, the Throat, the Third Eye and the Crown. From lower to higher, they symbolise a beautiful path of growth and development through life and form the foundation for the seven-step journey we took in the book *Lifting the Veils of Illusion*. We will revisit them on this journey of mastery as well. Yet, there are further chakras, and familiarity with the 12 chakra system will add depth, context, and appreciation to your understanding of how chakras work and how best to balance these refined energies in your life.

Although various teachers and writers may have mentioned these, the 12 chakra system is relatively new. The five higher chakras are only opening up to us now. They represent the next step of our evolution in this new era of enlightenment and exist at a more refined energy level. We are still discovering the nature, qualities and functions of the higher or Sacred Chakras, therefore there are numerous variations in understanding, description and colours allocated to the 12 chakras. They mostly involve the Earth Star Chakra below the feet, the Navel Chakra, the Higher Heart and two or more additional chakras above the Crown Chakra. As we take this 12-step journey, I will endeavour to describe the new chakras more in their broadest sense.

The metaphor of creation and evolution in colours below (see Figure 2), provides a natural framework for the colours of the chakras as I understand them. Even though the Sacred Chakras are new, they correlate beautifully with an ancient system. Diane Stein also points to this correlation in her description of the 12 chakra system as 'part of the ancient Chi Kung system, yet seem to be opening spontaneously for the first time in many people' (Stein, 1995). Like Diane, I too experience these Sacred Chakras starting to open up for my clients. We then work to clear and align these higher chakras. I see it as an essential part of your awakening and ascension process. Once opened, you can channel so much more light, activate your higher gifts, step into true mastery and fulfil your destiny as a lightworker (as described in *Lifting the Veils of Illusions, 7 Steps to Spiritual Enlightenment*) in this significant transitional time on

7

Earth. The five higher chakras are more etheric, subtle and spiritual of nature and can therefore be called Sacred Chakras. These higher Sacred Chakras are key to the work of mastery. Understanding their functions and working with them means you can now fulfil your own work of evolution and empowerment.

The 12 chakra system brings forth the vision of our connection to the entire universe. All living beings are part of a whole. Each of us is grounded to the Earth and energetically linked to the entire universe at the same time. Using the 12 chakra system allows you to draw from powerful energies outside of the human body and get in touch with the whole array of dimensions of your human experience.

There are other minor chakras in the energy system, each with their unique functions. Because they link up to the major chakras, this discussion will focus on the main 12 chakras so that you can understand and experience your whole energy system.

When these chakras are all activated, you become a brilliant channel of light. You can visualise yourself as a conduit of light, connecting deep into the core of the Earth and ascending into the highest dimension of light, connecting you to the divine source of the crystalline light.

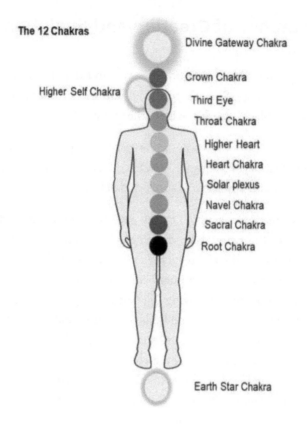

Figure 1: The 12 Chakras

Twelve Strands of DNA

As we activate the 12 chakras, we also reconnect the missing strands of DNA to bring the mind, body and soul back into wholeness and embody more light. Our current double-helix DNA contains the genetic code of life. Yet, two strands of DNA are quite limited in comparison to what we can access when all twelve strands are reconnected. As the DNA begins to form new strands, information and memories are unlocked, and you are restored to the light being you once were. This reconnection of your DNA to its full potential is happening right now through the activation of the 12 chakras.

A Metaphor of Creation and Evolution in Colour

In the beginning there was nothing – the no thing, the void, pure un-manifest energy. Something stirred and out of the void – the darkness, the black – came the light, the white.

And so out of the one whole, came the first separation, the first opposites, that of yin and yang. The One divides into two in order to create energy and opposites of above and below.

Unity gave birth to Duality. Duality gave birth to Trinity. Trinity gave birth to the many. Like dividing cells, separation continues further into ever-colourful diversity and variation. White light first fractionated into the three primary colours of red, blue and yellow. In the same way, the life-giving light of pure spirit manifests the three light bodies – the mental body, the emotional body and the etheric physical body. The light bodies fractionated again into a rainbow of seven colours and seven chakras with an infinite number of ever-separating shades and minor chakras. That's our descent into the world of concrete form in all its colourful array and diversity. Experience is gained here through all its variations.

Now, wisdom in hand, we're on the return path to wholeness, the path of ascension, back into the light. We gather and merge, we come together, bring together, stand together. We once were energy beings who descended into form. Now we ascend from form into energy beings again. Following the rainbow bridge into ever higher vibrational light where blue becomes light blue, red becomes pink and yellow becomes gold. From seven chakras to three *tan tiens* – your energy bodies of blue, pink and gold – your ascension vehicle. Light blue for the abdominal *tan tien* and etheric physical body. Pink for the higher heart and emotional body. Gold for the higher mind and mental body, an expression of your Higher Self, is a powerful healing light. Gold as the colour of the New Golden Era, represents a time when you can be the full magnificence of your Higher Self here on Earth. As above, so below. Colour is vibration. The ever lighter and brighter light eventually merges back into pure spirit of white light again. Finally, through the oval gateway; the zero point, into wholeness; the realm of infinite potential and infinite possibilities.

Figure 2: A Metaphor of Creation and Evolution in Colour

Out of the 0, the dark No Thing, came the One, the Light. Duality of yin and yang is born. Light fractionates in three primary colours, creating Trinity. Trinity fractionates in a rainbow of seven, then many infinite shades.

About the Book

Describing the Journey

We are about to embark on a journey through the 12 chakra system – an advanced journey of empowerment and fulfilment. We will revisit familiar and fundamental steps. We will also discover new and advanced steps. The concepts and processes in this book are powerful, transformational and designed to bring about shifts towards higher levels of consciousness. It's a journey of discovering your masterful self, so that you can open up to your higher gifts.

Each Step will explore the relevant chakra or energy centre, the related spiritual laws and powerful lessons of mastery. Each Step features practical self-empowering exercises and meditations with audio links. We will uncover your multi-dimensional self; the nature of your three minds, and your four energy bodies, as well as the various planes or dimensions of existence. We will explore the significance of our existence on earth during this time of a shift into a new era of enlightenment. Throughout the 12-Step process we will raise our conscious awareness and take in more light on the path which has ascension as its ultimate destination.

The 12-Step process is aimed at assisting you to navigate and accelerate your journey. So, enjoy your journey as you grow and evolve in mastery. This is the most significant journey of your life. It is essentially a journey back home. Enjoy the ride!

Step 1: Be the Master

Journey Through the Chakras: Base or Root Chakra

We start the journey grounded, rooted in power, purpose, health and vitality – a sound foundation for empowerment and advancement into mastery.

Colour	Red
Location	Pelvic area at the base of your spine
Qualities and Functions of the Root Chakra	Safety and security. The Root Chakra keeps you grounded, energised, present and healthy.
Key Functions for Mastery	• Purpose and power. • Grounding and protection. • Moving beyond fear and any need for security. • Embracing risk-taking and change. • Mastering the Universal Laws of Cause and Effect. • Discipline and Healing. • Taking charge of your health and wellness through energy practices.

Master the Key Basic Universal Laws

- *The Law of Cause and Effect*: The Law of Cause and Effect is a creative law, basically designed so that you may create and experience your desired reality – a reality not only for your personal well-being, but also for the advancement of others and humanity as a whole. Through the Law of Cause and Effect balance is maintained. The quality of your thoughts determines the quality of your experiences. You can choose to be proactive in your thinking and action, rather than reactive. When you consciously and intentionally send thoughts and feelings of harmony, peace, love, and light to people, places, or conditions, your soul, the Master Within, instantly aids you in your causative creation (Edwards, 2015).

- *The Law of Discipline*: By practising discipline, you expand yourself to a greater degree than almost any other action. Discipline is the surest means to greater freedom and independence. It provides the focus to achieve the skill level and depth of knowledge that translates into more options in life (Millman, 1993).

  Paradoxically, discipline may seem the opposite of freedom. The freedom to do as you please may feel more appealing. Discipline is the key to freedom, independence and true empowerment. It is through the discipline of doing that we reap fruit. The regular discipline of meditation over time will still the mind, focus thoughts, sharpen intuitive guidance, fill you with the light of enlightenment and bring you more in alignment with your true higher mind and your full potential.

- *The Law of Healing*: Healing takes place when one channels high-frequency energy; the light which radiates from source. By channelling this life force energy, blockages are removed and the body restored to its natural vitality. Blockages are caused by suppressed emotions, constricting insecurities, ego-driven conflict, fear and stress. Healing is wholeness. When you are of one integrated higher mind, you are whole and healthy. Your natural state is positivity, flow, joy, love and perfect health. Healing can be channelled in your meditation. Healing can be sent into the past, present and future. Healing can be sent to others provided you ask for permission, intending it to be for their highest and greater good. Ultimately, raised consciousness is your blueprint for perfect health, as discussed in Step 2.

Purpose

The Root Chakra forms a strong base from where to live your purpose. This is such a significant lifetime on Earth and we are transmuting a lot of karma. The purpose of life is to learn and evolve. Your purpose may be to finally overcome fear and limiting beliefs, claim your gift and step into your power. Many of us are here to heal family karma and bring to an end long-held family patterns such as anger, fear, hurt, judgements or addictions. Your purpose may be to heal blocked emotions, not just your own, but also healing your ancestral line in the process. Carl Jung believed that many karmic patterns are societal and have been passed down the generations (Snowden, 2010). Anything unresolved was passed on to be sorted out by the next generation. We live in a time of urgency to finally transmute these patterns, move beyond the wheel of karma and raise the consciousness of the whole. All consciousness is connected. As you let go of your own fears and limiting beliefs, you also help to heal the family and the world. Your purpose may be to free yourself from criticism and opinions and set yourself free to follow your own path. Your purpose may be to challenge existing societal beliefs and judgement about rights and wrongs and about what's 'normal'. As a change agent, you are here to assist in uplifting the consciousness of the whole into ever higher levels of awareness. We clothe ourselves in these patterns by being born in them. Then when we heal ourselves, we liberate the family and the collective.

Power

More than ever before, the world needs you to act from within your true power; your gift of greatness. We may be thinking of great leaders in history that displayed remarkable strength and power, such as Gandhi's power in gentleness that saved a nation, or Churchill who led the nation fearlessly during a time of war. This power and potential for greatness is in all of us. Now is the time to step into your true higher power for a higher purpose. Power is a strong foundation like that of a sturdy tree, solid and grounded. With power in the base, you can stand your ground, courageously and strong, while flexibly flowing with life, like willow branches in the wind, acting on your inner guidance in the moment. Embracing your true power is key to mastery so, we will explore power again in Step 3.

Beyond Fear Is Only Love

Here at the Root Chakra we face our most basic instinctual emotion of fear; our survival instincts and need for safety and security. Fear is the greatest of all illusions. Fear only exists in the mind. How often do we fear things that never happen? Thankfully 99 per cent of the time the things we fear never happen. We live in a world of duality. We gain insights through experiencing complete opposites such as day and night, light and dark, male and female, even concepts of good and bad or right and wrong. The ultimate duality is that of fear and love. All negative emotions and limiting beliefs stem from fear. All positive emotions and experiences are love-based. Perlmutter and Villoldo (2011) describe the old reptilian instinctual brain that triggers the fight or flight response. This brain was useful at a time when we lived in a jungle where survival was its main motivation. We are now evolving beyond this fear-based world view, its suffering and its fight and flight response. It has become obsolete. Beyond fear is relaxation, creativity, infinite potential, joy and love. We have a choice. The old instinctual brain can still trigger for no reason. It's up to us now to choose between the way of fear or the way of love. Through choice and disciplined thought, the old reactive brain can be de-energised and the higher brain of creativity, consciousness, health, joy and wisdom can be energised and strengthened. We can now end the suffering consciousness and wilfully train the brain to facilitate enlightened consciousness. Recognise the fear response and the old suffering programme, intentionally de-energise them and open up to love, creativity and wisdom – your true natural state.

Mastery is freedom from fear

The Root-based energy-vibration of safety, security and stability is fear-based, constrictive and stagnant. Concepts of safety, security and stability are illusions created by the ego to keep your reality limited to a three-dimensional existence.

The universe loves the energy of risk-taking. Risk backed up by faith and trust, is a massive injection of energy – an energy that will return to you multi-fold. For every action there is an equal and opposite reaction. This is Newton's Third Law of Motion, and is the Law of Cause and Effect by another description. By the Law of Cause and Effect, the more you put in, the more the universe gives you in return. Ultimately, the Law of Cause and Effect teaches us that we are accountable for our own circumstances and the actions we take. The Cause aspect of this Law implies choice, creativity, empowerment and positive action. Put that in, and the Effect you'll experience will be success, growth and expansion.

Change is inevitably part of life and evolution. Motion is built into the fabric of the universe. Nothing stays still. Embrace change as essential for your growth. Resistance to change causes suffering and can manifest in the body as stiffness, rigidness and even arthritis.

Surrendering to change and flowing with life is crucial for your health and well-being.

You may encounter fear in its many forms further along the various steps in the book. Recognise the fear, see it as an opportunity for transformation. Learn from it and intentionally release any fear, so that you can finally move beyond fear into love, creativity, joy and expansion.

The Mastermind-set

Taking Full Responsibility

I am 100 per cent responsible for my health, my relationship, my perceptions, beliefs, thoughts, choices and outcomes. I take full responsibility for what I create and experience in my universe. By taking full responsibility, I come into my full power. This insight and power, I can use to accelerate my growth and evolution. As I accelerate my evolution, I uplift the whole.

Recognising the Illusion

As I remain the observer, I can see through the illusion of the three-dimensional world of the fearful ego. I can choose the true reality of love every time, embracing the experience of life. I embrace the creative energy of risk-taking. I open to life and flow with change.

Everything Is Energy

Energy has quantity and quality. I can imprint a quality into energy with thoughts. As an example, I can visualise filling myself up with the optimum quantity of healing energy and imprint with thought-intention into the energy the quality of joy for life.

Mastery Practices

Our everyday work, interactions with people, thoughts, emotions, concerns and stresses, can leave us feeling drained and energetically flat. If we don't do something to rebalance ourselves, this energy drain can impact on our mood and on the physical body in the form of aches, pains and even illness. There is so much you can do to restore and rebalance yourself. Master these subtle, simple and easy energy practices and pro-actively take charge of your own good health.

Grounding

The pressures of modern life keep us very much in the mind – thinking ahead, planning, stressing; or going over the past – analysing, regretting, blaming. When we're in the head, we're not really in the body. We're not present in the moment. In contrast, the present moment is completely free from stress. Planning and evaluating has its place, but life can only be lived in the present moment. Mindfulness practices enables us to get out of the mind and live life through our senses. Through grounding we bring the mind and our awareness back to the body so that we can be here, present in the moment, enjoying life as a sense-experience. An easy grounding practice (preferably done outside), is to feel your bare feet connected and rooted to the Earth. This connection in itself is very nourishing, cleansing and energising. As time speeds up and the energies become more high vibrational, it will be even more important to stay grounded. Make grounding your regular foundational practice. Grounding through your Earth Star Chakra will be described in Step 8. As you reconnect to the Earth's sacred healing energy, you become solidly grounded, deeply nourished and recharged. You can also discharge into the earth any excess energy.

Protection

As you surely have experienced, your energy can get drained and contaminated. It is therefore essential that you protect yourself energetically. You can protect yourself through a simple practice of intention setting, visualising your light being shielded. The idea of protection per se has an underlying fear vibration. As a master, stay free from fear and remain in your true power. At the same time remain streetwise in the world of energy to optimise your own energetic health.

What we send out in the world, will, by the Laws, return to us. Here's a key mastery principle: There is nothing outside of you that isn't you. Ultimately, we protect ourselves from ourselves; from what we send out, and which, by the Laws, will return to us in similar form. If we send out fear and mistrust, we will attract situations that perpetuate fear and mistrust. The best form of protection is thus mindfulness of the thoughts, emotions and energies that you send out. When you place yourself in the light and in loving vibrations, love and positivity will radiate from you and will return to you.

Clearing

Are you one of those people to whom others come with their stories, seeking advice or just offloading? Interaction with people can be uplifting at times and at other times it can leave you feeling energetically drained or contaminated. Have you ever visited a chaotic shopping centre or made a visit to the hospital and came back home feeling drained? The laws of energy are similar to the natural laws. If you open a canal lock, water will naturally flow from the higher level to the lower level until it is at the same level. Similarly, when you are buzzing with energy and then interact with someone low in energy, they may leave buzzing and you just feel empty. Emotions are contagious. It's natural to take on emotions and energy of others during your daily interactions. Just make sure you clear yourself of it again. You can clear yourself of residual dense energy through your grounding practices, much in the way electricity is balanced by earthing it. Meditation is another way of clearing the mind, creating stillness and refreshing your energy.

Cleansing

In the world of energy, much can be done through visualisation and intention. When you shower or bath, you can intend that you cleanse your energy field and refresh yourself mentally, emotionally and physically. In a meditative state, visualise a cleansing light showering down on you, cleansing the body and the energy field around you. Give your gadgets a break. The electromagnetic smog they emanate impacts on your energy levels. Spring-clean your house, clean your car and declutter with intent. Your mind will feel all the clearer for it.

The inside creates the outside and the outside impacts the inside

Letting Go

Negative thoughts and low, or fearful or angry emotions can sap your energy. The simple practice of letting go can be very healing. Releasing the thoughts and emotions through intent, can make you feel lighter. This is another purpose of meditation. In your meditation, reflect on the issues of the day, learn from them and then intentionally let them go. This way you can put the day to bed and tomorrow can be a whole new beginning, a clean slate. This is the beauty of life: every day can be a new beginning.

Cutting Cords

The ancient people of Hawaii had a great understanding of energy. They taught that during our interaction with other people, we connect energetically through the auras. Connections are made through rapport, touch, strong feelings, strong thoughts and communication (even on the phone). If you have many such connections open, your energy can feel scattered and drained. A powerful healing meditation to cut the energy cords after you have interacted with people, is the Huna practice called *Ho'oponopono* described in Step 4. Use this fairly frequently to clear any thoughts or emotions after intense interactions, to let go of people on your mind, to cut cords and bring your energy back intact. Sometimes you have to say no to some of the demands people place on you, so that you can restore yourself and create balance between others' needs and your own.

Refreshing

Many energy practices such as yoga and tai chi have the purpose of cleansing, refreshing and re-energising your energy. Walking in nature can be equally refreshing. Nature is naturally cleansing. When you walk near water or trees, you can intend that your mind clears, that thoughts wash away and that your aura is cleansed in the breeze.

Re-energising

There is much you can do to re-energise yourself. We get energy physically from the food we eat, water we drink, sunlight and exercise. One of the most effective ways of re-energising yourself is through diaphragmatic breathing practices – another purpose of meditation. Breath is life. As long as we breathe we are alive! Breath is energy. Through breathing we generate energy. Breath is spirit. As we breathe in – inspire – we enliven ourselves.

The Benefits of Breathing

The simple practice of deep breathing is the most effective way to:

- Energise yourself.
- Detoxify: 70 per cent of toxins in the body are released through breathing.
- Relax: a longer out-breath, like a sigh, relaxes the nervous system.
- Slow your heart rate.
- Raise your energy to higher vibrations and you feel uplifted.
- Clear the mind.
- Align your mind, body and soul.
- Restore balance.

Meditation

The mind and the body are linked. From a cause and effect perspective, the mind is the cause and the body the effect. Working at the physical level is rather like putting a plaster on a wound. Although there are times when it's helpful to bring comfort to the body, it's best to approach your health from a mental and emotional level. Recreating good health energetically, soon manifests as physical good health. Follow this powerful self-healing meditation to check in on your health, physically, emotionally, mentally and energetically and be the master of your own health.

During the meditations to follow, we will connect and work with our protector and healing guides. If you are not yet familiar with the concept of guides, follow the 'Meditation to Connect with your Guides' as described in *Lifting the Veils of Illusion, 7 Steps to Spiritual Enlightenment.*

Visit
www.brightfuturenow.co.uk/meditations
to download or listen to a free audio meditation:
Meditation to Connect with Your Guides

Advanced Self-Healing Meditation

- Ground, protect, connect with your healing guides and Higher Self.
- Scan how you feel emotionally; scan the nature of the thoughts on your mind.
- How do these emotions and thoughts impact the brightness of your energy field?
- Become aware of your own energy field, your aura. See it or feel it as an oval bubble of light about an arms-length all around you.
- Scan your aura up and down, front and back and to the sides. Is the left side and right side the same, or is one side more expanded than the other? As you trace your aura, you can also intentionally expand out both sides, so that they are the same. Now, scan for any darker areas. Is the energy around your head clear and light or does it feel like a grey cloud created by thought forms?

- Scan the rest of the energy field for darker spots or stains caused by feelings, stress, interactions or experiences.
- Do the scanning effortlessly. Let the picture form all by itself, let the colours and intuition just come to you. You can also ask your healing guides to show you what you need to be aware of.
- Now, ask your healing guides and Higher Self to step in and assist you. Your Higher Self is your ultimate healer, so as you set intention, you receive assistance.
- Set the intention to release any negative emotions like anger or fear. Ask for assistance with this.
- Set the intention for the release of any self-limiting beliefs or anxious thoughts.
- Intend, visualise and ask that any thought forms and contamination that may have accumulated and built up in your aura as a result of your experiences be removed.
- Tune into your energy field and sense the experience. Witness the process of cleansing. Sense the release.
- Intend and visualise that any energy cords that may still connect you to others energetically, be dissolved.
- Intend and visualise an energy cleanse like a shower of cleansing light, sense it.
- Intend and visualise an energy balance; that the chakra system be recalibrated and realigned – this can take ten minutes.
- Stay attuned, sensing, witnessing, breathing a cleansing breath, staying present and connected, feeling gratitude.
- Intend and visualise your aura being filled with bright white or golden light. You may even intend the light to contain the quality of positive resources such as joy and love.
- Intend, visualise and ask that any tears or weak areas in the aura, the result of daily stresses, interactions and experiences, be repaired and strengthened.

- Thank your guides, ask for protection, that this new light and energy be sealed in.
- Ground.

Visit
www.brightfuturenow.co.uk/meditations
to download or listen to a free audio meditation:
Advanced Self-healing Meditation

Step 2: Master Your Emotions

Continuing to lay a sound foundation for mastery, in Step 2 we will explore foundational principles of mindfulness as a way of broadening our awareness and observing our habitual emotional and mental patterns. Emotional levels are great indicators of levels of consciousness and by embracing our emotions we can heal and climb the vibrational ladder of consciousness.

Journey Through the Chakras: Sacral Chakra

Colour	Orange
Location	Below the navel
Qualities and Functions of the Sacral Chakra	Sacral Chakra is the centre of creativity, sexuality, family and social relationships. It's the centre of our emotions and our ability to bring abundance into the world.
Key Functions for Mastery	• Creativity, emotional health and raised consciousness. • Bringing mindfulness to your emotions. • Moving to the higher vibrations of love and joy. • Embracing your creative energy to bring forth abundance into the world. • Mastering the Universal Laws of Awareness.

Master the Key Universal Laws of Awareness

- *The Law of Non-judgement*: judgement is a human invention of duality.
- *The Law of Non-attachment*: let be; let go.
- *The Law of Reflection*: we are always looking in a mirror.
- *The Law of Vibration*: your emotions are indicators of your consciousness at the time.

Anxiety, Stress and Depression: Our Modern-Day Illnesses

People come for therapy increasingly because they experience anxiety and depression. There is so much happening so fast. People feel overwhelmed by increased responsibilities and demands on their time and resources. Pressure can be felt at work, from financial commitments and family responsibilities. So much is changing all the time. We have to keep up with technology and social media. Technology keeps us indoors, separating us from nature and from a true sense of community interaction. At the root of stress is fear. We fear not having enough, not doing what we want to do, not being who we think we should be. The news media bring issues from all over the world into our living rooms, over-stimulating the mind, creating nervous energy. The fears that rise aren't always your fears. They are collective fears. The Sacral energy is tribal energy. The tribe can have expectations and expressed opinions about your roles and responsibilities. The tribe can also experience stress when you break away and follow your own path. By its nature, the tribe is invested in maintaining the tribe. Following your own inner radar will fill you with the dynamic energy to create your own destiny. This implies cutting through all the expectations, roles and responsibilities. Beyond fear, within each of us, is a space of innate well-being and peace. That's where you want to dwell and from there you want to flow your creativity in your own unique way. Your inner radar is often emotion-driven. Your feelings are subtle messages, so it's worth tuning in and listening.

The world of your emotions can be mysterious and bizarre, so how can you approach your emotions wisely?

Mysterious Facts about the Nature and Functions of your Emotions

It's Real

Accept what you feel as real. Your feelings are more real than your thoughts. They rise from a place of your authentic self. You are human after all, so tune into your feelings. The knowing and accepting of the feeling is the seed of wisdom and good health. Give yourself permission to feel your feelings. Honouring your feelings means you are heeding a call from your deeper unconscious.

It's All Linked

Emotions are stored like clusters of similar types (anger or fear) in the unconscious mind, which is why they tend to accumulate and grow stronger. The bag gets full. When you experience a new event causing you fear, it brings up all past fears because the mind associates the new event with past experiences of the same emotion. In therapy, we always look for the root cause; the start of the cluster. That way, we can get to the bottom of it and release the entire cluster. The result is like a good cleanse, the bag gets emptied and you feel much lighter, at peace and you can move ahead.

It's Unconscious

The unconscious mind represses memories with unresolved negative emotions. These could be emotionally traumatic events. It does this for your own protection; to help you get through your day or get on with life. Often in discussion about past events, clients will

29

say to me: Oh I've dealt with that. It doesn't bother me anymore. They think they've dealt with it, but instead they've packed it away. Stored emotions are chemicals in the cells and can create physical discomfort and health conditions over time. Stress hormones are an example familiar to most of us.

It's Irrational

Your emotional unconscious mind works radically different from your logical rational mind. There's nothing rational about emotions. It's completely irrational. It's still real though. Phobias are classic examples. People with phobias such as fear of open spaces, public speaking, failure, buttons, birds, and the like, say they know it's irrational and yet they still feel it. Your unconscious mind, being irrational, may pick strange moments to bring up repressed memories for emotional healing and releasing. It gauges, in its own irrational way, that you are ready to face the feelings and deal with it. It may happen when you least expect it. Mastery is attending to whatever arises, healing and releasing it.

It's Like Water

E-motion is energy in motion. Emote means to flow through and out. Healthy emotions have the same fluidity as water. Emotions need to flow through you, and expression is a way of doing it. From a therapeutic perspective, emotions aren't a problem unless they are unresolved, accumulated or suppressed. Saying how you feel can educate those around you and they can get to know you better.

It's a Coded Language

As with pain in the body, our emotions are really messages from the unconscious mind. These aren't always immediately obvious, yet there's a lot to learn from them. Anger for example, can mean that someone may have overstepped a boundary and that it may be time to re-assert your boundaries. Anxiety tells us that the mind is focusing on what we don't want to happen, rather than what we do want. What we focus on expands, so ironically, when we focus on a potential negative outcome, we energise and expand the possibility of the undesirable thing happening. Sadness and depression can be the result of unexpressed anger, now turned inward. If this continues over a prolonged period, it can impact on the body physically. Reflection shines a light of clarity into the murky waters of the unconscious mind. Then the waters can clear and wisdom can shine through.

It's Your Friend

Ultimately, your emotions serve as a gateway to your intuitive self and by befriending your emotions, honouring and valuing them, you can access your own inner wisdom. The more you attend to your emotions as subtle messages, the stronger your intuitive ability grows. This way you are more in touch with your inner guidance and that is a priceless gift.

It's Contagious

Emotions are contagious and tend to rub off onto others. Your unconscious mind – your emotional mind – is very sensitive and picks up very easily on the subtleties of feelings of the people around you. In fact, it doesn't really distinguish between your feelings and mine. They all become intertwined and connected as one, because at the level of the unconscious mind, we are one. So, we can be dragged down or uplifted. Equally, we can have a dulling or uplifting effect on others. Being aware of this gives us choices.

Emotions Have Vibrations

We have all walked into a room and sensed the 'vibes'. You can feel the tension or the lightness. Emotions have vibrations. Some, like stress and fear, are dense and low in vibration, causing tension. Others, like love and joy, are light and high in vibration. Higher vibrations are naturally more uplifting and expansive (Hawkins, 1995).

It's a Human Experience

It is natural and human to experience the whole range of emotions. One day you may feel optimistic and positive, and then comes a day when you feel low for no apparent reason. Instead of resisting the lower emotions, be willing to experience the whole range of human emotions. What you resist persists. Equally, avoid dwelling in the lower emotions. Here we may experience blame or resistance or force or struggle against the flow of life. Instead, flow through the experience with awareness and intention to move back up into positive emotions. Releasing resistance and taking responsibility begins to tip us into positive emotions. Practising acceptance, gratitude and forgiveness helps us to transcend the ego and become more of our true higher selves. Clarity brings wisdom and previously evasive emotions of unconditional love, joy and peace are experienced again as our true natural state. Youthfulness and good health – also our natural state – return.

It's an Indicator of Consciousness

Emotional levels are levels of consciousness. Where you dwell in emotions, you dwell in consciousness. Consciousness (not DNA) controls the health in your body as well as your levels of success in achieving positive outcomes. Consciousness changes and activates your DNA, allowing more of your resources and potential to be tapped. Consciousness is your blueprint for health and success (Edwards, 2010).

The Link Between Emotions, Health and Success

As is evident from the emotional scale in Table 1 below, if you dwell in lower emotions too long, you can experience apathy and your energy becomes more constrictive and solid. You can't make decisions because you resist change. You want things to stay the same. You want to BE right. You take life too seriously and are motivated by safety and security. Stress and fear make you ill. You feel like a victim of circumstances, as though life is unfair. You can drag people down with you. People around you can find you draining. People at these levels tend to be risk-averse. They remember past failures and generate a lot of 'what if' type mental chatter. Ironically, the more we focus on the negative, the more it expands in possibility and prevalence.

Higher up in positive emotions of willingness, gratitude, excitement and enthusiasm, there's more movement and flow in energy. You become more expansive and you have more space to create. You are driven by vision and purpose, rather than money. You feel energised and healthy. It's easier to come into your own power, to be creative and to manifest positive outcomes. Abundance is a natural outflow. People who cultivate positivity and dwell higher up the emotional levels, are playful and happy. They don't take life too seriously. They take full responsibility for their own experiences. They have a contagious enthusiasm. They have strong positive intentions. They want to DO right. They feel inspired and serve as an inspiration to others.

Your health and success depend on your willingness to:
- Experience the whole range of human emotions – rather than resist them
- Embrace and flow with the emotions you experience – rather than trying to control them
- Learn from the experience, let it go and then intentionally move up the emotional scale
- Practise forgiveness, gratitude, willingness, enthusiasm and positive intention
- Keep creating to expand (your business, career or personal empowerment)
- Remain light-hearted and playful
- Remain vision and purpose driven – abundance will flow by itself.

Emotions Have Vibrations

Table 1: Emotional Scale of Vibrations

Vibration	Emotional Levels	Qualities of Consciousness
	Positive	**True Higher Self**
700–1,000	Enlightenment	Playful, happy
600	Peace, bliss	Able to create and manifest
540	Joy, excitement, enthusiasm	Expansive, abundant
500	Unconditional love	Powerful, empowered
400	Reason, clarity, understanding	Energising
350	Acceptance, forgiveness	Inspirational
310	Gratitude, positivity, optimism	Driven by purpose and vision
250	Willingness, trust, satisfaction	Taking responsibility
200	Courage, affirmation	Flow, flexibility
	Negative	**Ego Self**
175	Pride, self-righteousness	Serious
150	Anger, resentment, jealousy, control	Constrictive, resistant
125	Desire, addiction, disappointment	Forceful
100	Fear, worry, doubt	Draining
75	Grief	Motivated by safety and security
50	Apathy	Victimhood
30	Guilt	Avoid decisions
20	Shame	Resist change, rigid, solid

Inspired by: David R. Hawkins (1995) and Gill Edwards (2010)

Consciousness is your blueprint for health and success

The Mastermind-set

- I embrace all my emotions and keep moving towards love and joy.
- I mindfully tune into my feelings, to learn from them and grow in wisdom.

The foundational principles of mindfulness, which is practised widely now, has its origin in Buddhism. These principles, although challenging, can be very helpful in broadening our awareness and observing our habitual emotional and mental patterns. They can also help us to remain non-reactive in situations that are emotionally charged, offering us a way to remain calm and clear. Mindfulness as a practice will be revisited in Step 5.

1. Non-Judging

Our tendency to label or judge events, people and experiences as good or bad, right or wrong, liking or disliking, exciting or boring, fair or unfair, or can do or can't do, is simply an ego presumption. When we stop labelling or judging, we can become the impartial witness and accept everything just as a learning experience. If we have the tendency to judge others, we will certainly judge ourselves too. Monitor that critical voice in your head and stop any self-judgement. When you do, you will stop judging others and they will stop judging you. Work on replacing the critical voice with a compassionate voice that gently and lovingly furthers your growth.

2. Patience

Be patient with your own experience – with what is happening in this moment – instead of rushing to the next. Live in the here and now. Patience is a form of wisdom. Let everything unfold in its own time. The butterfly can't be helped out of a chrysalis.

3. Acceptance

Acceptance doesn't mean liking or giving up or satisfied, it just means non-resistance and accepting what is right now as a starting point. Acceptance is a precondition for healing. Acceptance brings peace. Embrace acceptance and compassion as opportunities for mastery. Accept that everyone is on their own unique path of experience and growth.

4. Non-Attachment

We create our own suffering by holding onto things or wanting things to be different from what they are. We want to hang onto pleasure and avoid pain. We hang onto summer and the holiday and dreading winter and going back to work. Just let your experience be as it is. Notice and let go. Let go of the attachment to specific outcomes as well. That is a habit of control. Accept and let go of everything. Let go like you do when you go to sleep at night. Then you can start the new day afresh and free.

5. Letting Go

Set the intention to let it go. Releasing brings relief and makes space for joy to return.

Let go emotionally; of any unsettling feelings, and mentally; of excessive thoughts. Let go of the need to control too. A major source of suffering is wanting things 'my way'. Everything happens for your own learning and growth. Let go of the importance of other people's opinions too. They are just opinions, not truths. When you attach too much value to their opinions, you are giving your power away. Liberate yourself from others' opinions and give yourself the permission to just be your true self. That brings freedom and happiness.

6. Non-Doing

Our continuous busy-ness can create stress and overthinking. Our minds become cluttered, forgetful and confused. Taking time to just be, can be very nourishing and refreshing. It is like a reset for the mind and brings much-needed clarity. With the left thinking brain quieting, the right creative brain can open up. Daydreaming is a great way of just being. As you daydream, you just follow the natural trail of your thoughts as they flow into new creative ideas and perspectives. In the relaxed state of daydreaming, the mind opens up to the subtlety of intuition, inspiration and inner wisdom – the seat of creativity.

7. Connectedness

Awareness of our intrinsic wholeness and interconnectedness offers us a new approach to emotions. Emotions are contagious and it's easy to feel others' fear, sadness and anger. Equally, when you are calm, at peace, loving and joyful, you bring a beautiful gift of upliftment to others.

8. Wakefulness

Present moment awareness is a great mastery practice. Most people go through life and their daily routine in a trance, asleep, unaware, on automatic pilot. When we are present in the moment, we are truly alive and awakened.

Bronnie Ware, a palliative care nurse in Australia, routinely asked her patients about their regrets. In her book *The Top Five Regrets of the Dying* (2012), she records the following common regrets:

1. I wish I'd dared to live a life true to myself, not the life others expected of me (pursuing your own dreams).
2. I wish I hadn't worked so hard (work–life balance).
3. I wish I'd dared to express my feelings (honouring and expressing your feeling positively impacts your health and happiness).
4. I wish I had stayed in touch with my friends (personal connections make life meaningful).
5. I wish that I had let myself be happier (happiness is a choice regardless of circumstances).

***

When you are by the sea, watch the waves on the seashore.
Waves like thoughts and feelings, they roll in they roll out.
Sometimes big sometimes small.
We can't stop them so watch them, appreciate them, witness
their rise and fall.
Notice what happens when you do.
Notice the mindful moments of stillness.
Notice what happens when you pay attention to what is
happening, when it is happening.
Without having a need for it be one way or another way.
Ask yourself 'Am I fully awake in this moment?'

Reflections by Lou Booth, Wellness Coach and Mindfulness
Practitioner

***

Mastery Practices

- Embrace acceptance and compassion as opportunity for mastery.
- Remain the wise observer.
- Embrace your creative energy to manifest abundance.
- To stay emotionally healthy, practise a daily reflection. Every experience, even the challenges and so-called mistakes, have been part of your growth. A key practice in Transformational Therapy is to reflect on the learning experiences of past events. You can do your own daily reflection by asking yourself:
  - What was good about today?
  - What was not so good?
  - What am I learning from it?
  - What will I do different next time?

- Then after your reflection, let it go. Sometimes you may have to bring compassion and forgiveness to yourself and others. You will feel a weight lifting and the release can be very healing.
- Understanding the vibrational energies of thoughts and feelings, keep moving to higher vibrations.
- Practise gratitude daily. This powerful practice creates a positive mental shift every time. Gratitude activates neurotransmitters serotonin and dopamine which are powerful natural anti-depressants. Start a gratitude journal and capture three things every day for which you are grateful. This simple practice has an immediate uplifting impact and is a highly effective way of moving up the emotional scale into positive emotions.
- Bring gratitude into a mindfulness meditative practice. Reflect firstly, on a person you are grateful for, secondly, an event you are grateful for, thirdly, something about yourself you are grateful for. In your meditation, focus on the feeling of gratitude rather than the story.

Visit
www.brightfuturenow.co.uk/meditations
to download or listen to a free audio meditation:
Gratitude Meditation

Ultimately, we heal by connecting with our soul

Meditation

Higher Self-Healing Meditation
A powerful and sacred meditation for healing and releasing emotions of fear, anger, sadness, hurt, shame and guilt.

- Ground, connect with your guides and set the intention for protection by placing yourself in the light.

- Sit in your own space, breathing.
- Pay attention to your body, emotions, how are you feeling? Honour it, feel it.
- Following your inner guidance and identify the root cause of the emotion.
- It may go way back to childhood events.
- It may run in the family and go back over generations.
- It may have past life memory coming up for you.
- Ask to be guided to the root cause and follow your intuitive guidance. Go with what comes up first.
- Reflect on it and learn from it.
- Then set the intention to release the emotion.
- Now bring your awareness in your heart; breathe to raise your vibration.
- Visualise a golden bubble of light above your head – the light of your Higher Self.
- Bring it down as a column of light into your body, fill yourself with the light of your Higher Self.
- Enjoy the colours, energy sensation, and feelings of love, joy, compassion and peace.
- Communicate with your Higher Self and your healing guides.
- Ask your Higher Self to come in and release the entire cluster of emotion.
- Pay attention to the emotions and notice the feeling when the emotions disappear.
- Ask your Higher Self to activate your higher gifts in you to assist you in future situations. These gifts may be an inner strength, wisdom to discern, higher vision, perspective, higher power, compassion, love and forgiveness.
- Meditate in the energy of your Higher Self, your source of perfect health, higher knowledge and peace for a while.
- Close down, stay connected, seal in the light and ground yourself.

Visit
www.brightfuturenow.co.uk/meditations
to download or listen to a free audio meditation:
Higher Self-healing Meditation

Step 3: Master the Art of Creation and Manifestation

Having released negative emotions and limiting beliefs in Step 2, you are ready to own your creative power and use it purposefully to create desired outcomes and co-create for the greater good of all.

Master the Universal Laws of Creation

- *The Law of Attention*: Energy follows thought. Whatever you focus on expands.
- *The Law of Intention*: Intention releases a universal force that makes things happen.
- *The Law of Manifestation*: Follow your inner guidance to manifest for the highest good.
- *The Law of Abundance*: Abundance is your birth right. The Universe is abundant by nature. Abundance means flowing with love, joy, happiness, vitality, laughter, generosity and all the good of life.
- *The Law of Flow*: Flow with life and your inner guidance in the moment and all good things will come to you. Give to receive. Flow your creative energy.

Journey Through the Chakras: Solar Plexus Chakra

Colour	Yellow
Location	Above the navel
Qualities and Functions of the Solar Plexus Chakra	Confidence, self-esteem, inner power, assertiveness, healthy ego and healthy boundaries. The name implies the sun within. Here is where you want to radiate and shine. The sun inside you empowers you to be who you are and to manifest creatively. Here you come into your own right and fulfil a healthy ego. Only from the basis of a healthy, fulfilled ego, can you begin to move beyond your ego into your greater self and reach out to others, working for the greater good in unity and wholeness. The fire of the Solar Plexus gives you the initiative, motivation, drive, enthusiasm and passion to work for what you believe in. This is the fire of transformation that turns watery emotions into strength and anger into compassion. The energy of anger in the positive is assertiveness – standing in your own power.
Key Functions for Mastery	• Knowing thyself; embracing and living your own uniqueness. • Being a masterful creator. • Embracing your true higher power for a higher purpose. • Coming into alignment and co-creating for the greater good of all. • Mastering the Laws of Creation, Manifestation and Abundance. • Moving beyond any perceived limitations and unleashing your unlimited creative potential.

Step into Your Power

Owning your power is such a key aspect of mastery, yet the concept is so often misunderstood. Let's explore the concept of power and the true meaning of it.

What is this Power?

It Is Not:

- *Force, or arrogance*: That's ego power.
- *Power over people*: That's despotism.

It Is:

- *Love*: Songs have been written about the power of love.
- *Gentleness*: There is great power in gentleness.
- *Your greatness*: Your true magnificence.

Why Are We So Scared of This Power?

We seem to carry a deep-seated unconscious fear of power inside of us. This may be because power has been abused in the past. Marianne Williamson (1992) wrote: 'Our deepest fear is not that we are inadequate. Our deepest fear is that we are powerful beyond measure. It is our light, not our darkness, that most frightens us... Your playing small doesn't serve the world... As we are liberated from our own fear, we unconsciously give other people permission to do the same'.

It may be that power has been misused in history, yet imagine the magic when this power is used for the greater good, the betterment, upliftment, enlightenment and positive evolution of all life on Earth.

Own Your Power

You can't use your power until you've owned it. Recognise that this power is in you anyway. The only thing that obscures it is our own fears and limiting beliefs – fears of opinions, criticism, rejection or hurt, and limiting beliefs that keep you in your ordinariness, rather than your greatness. Whatever you think you are, you are always more than that. You have infinite potential and untapped resources already inside you. Release any fears and doubts about who you are and what you are capable of. Every time you release a limiting belief (sometimes we do it by facing the fear and doing it anyway) life responds to you in magical ways and whole new dimensions of possibilities open up to you.

Power in Connection

As the old values of competitiveness and exploitation fall away, we find more and more the incredible power in community, collaboration, mutual support and joint endeavours for the greater good. The power of true connection can be so great, it can bring powerful healing.

Power with Vulnerability

Power and vulnerability paradoxically can coexist. As you recognise your power, acknowledge and accept your vulnerability and that of others. You are still human, take care of yourself physically, emotionally, spiritually and energetically.

Power with Humility

The ego loves power as well, but does not know humility. Power with humility is a quality of spirit; a quality only your true Higher Self can muster. When you tap in to the true power of your Higher Self, you discover a paradoxical humility at the same time.

Power for Purpose

When you tap into your true power, you tap into something that is you and at the same time greater than you. This universal force wants to flow through you. When you release the constricted power of the small ego self, you open up to a vast expansive power, that of your greater true self. The ego self; the personality self, is the outer show. The true self is the inner strength. Your true Higher Self is beyond any perceived limitations, experiences the oneness of everything and emanates love, joy and peace. When you flow with this strength and power, you can tap into your true purpose and live your purpose powerfully.

What Do I Do with This Power?

Create: Be the all-powerful creator that you are.

Heal: Your life, your family and the world.

Bring change: Be the change agent, ushering in a peaceful, loving world.

Take action: Act with certainty and commitment to your chosen path.

Inspire others effortlessly: Through just being who you are and doing what you do.

Step into your greater purpose powerfully: Be the master, the creator, the lightworker and change agent the world needs right now. That's what you came to do.

You can't use your power until you've owned it

The Mastermind-set

- I embrace and live my own uniqueness.
- I am a powerful creator. Aligned, I co-create for the greater good of all.
- I embrace true higher power for a higher purpose.
- Know Thyself. This phrase is attributed to the Greek philosopher Socrates and is inscribed in the forecourt of the Temple of Apollo at Delphi. Some Eastern philosophies behold that one's entire life is a journey towards self-discovery. Therapy and self-development courses provide us with a platform to know ourselves. It's not just knowing ourselves intellectually or emotionally. It is knowing the greatness of your true self. This true self, and its infinite potential, are best discovered in the silence of contemplation and meditation. Your true Higher Self is the source of your inner strength and greater power. Your Higher Self knows your life's purpose. Great wisdom and guidance can be tapped here.

Mastery Practices

- Move beyond any perceived limitations and unleash your unlimited creative potential.
- Set your intentions for every activity daily. This way you create your desired outcomes ahead of you and keep your mind focused on what you want.

- Bring manifestation into your meditation to realise your goals.
- Keep creating through intention and visualisation.

The Keys to Masterful Manifestation

You are essentially a creator. As you think, so you create. Now that we are moving into the higher refined energy vibrations of a fifth-dimensional New Earth (as described in Step 8), everything is speeding up. Thoughts manifest much quicker. Fifth-dimensional manifestation is fast, so be aware of your thoughts (more on the nature of your thoughts in Step 5).

Know your Minds to Create in Synergy

Your three minds work together in the creation process, each with their own unique function. Knowledge of the nature and functions of your three minds and how they work together is key to manifesting masterfully.

Your Conscious Mind

This is your logical, rational thinking mind – the mind that analyses and processes information. With your Conscious Mind you make decisions, first the big picture and then the specifics and the details. Conscious focus energises and drives your intention and actions. Of the three minds, it is more limited and slower in the way it operates. Your Conscious Mind takes linear steps. One thing follows the next. It takes time to process. Your Conscious Mind is limited in how much information it can hold in conscious memory and what it can do in any given time. Your Conscious Mind is your three-dimensional focus, yet it clearly serves an important purpose. Your Conscious Mind directs the Unconscious Mind with intention, specific details and focus.

Your Unconscious Mind

Radically different in nature, your Unconscious Mind is your emotional mind, your feelings and intuition. There is nothing rational about this mind, yet it is very creative. It is more infinite and magical, yet childlike – the inner child. It needs guidance and direction from the Conscious Mind, like a child needs guidance from a parent. Highly suggestible, it picks up on every thought, hidden suggestion and intention, and creates your outcomes accordingly. That's why your emotions are a great indicator of the quality of your thoughts. Assist your inner child with positive, uplifting, encouraging thoughts. The resultant good mood builds positive self-esteem and a sense of well-being. Then your Unconscious Mind is best empowered and motivated to create your positive desired outcomes. Your Unconscious Mind runs your body, your health and stores your memory. It remembers everything. It also runs your programmes, habits, perceptions and beliefs, which can be changed by working with your Unconscious Mind. Whilst your Conscious Mind can only focus on one thing at a time, your Unconscious Mind's awareness is everywhere all of the time. Two million bits of information per second comes in through the senses – too much for the Conscious Mind to process. Your Unconscious Mind only passes through what it thinks is important to you – a mere 134 bits of information per second. When you set a goal or intention, you redirect the Unconscious Mind's radar to scan for information, resources and opportunities related to your new goal. This radar is called the Reticular Activating System – a network of nerve cells directing your attention to what is important to you.

Your unconscious mind operates in the fourth dimension with its quantum mechanical rules. Instead of linear steps, it takes a quantum leap to create outcomes fast and magically – in ways you may not have thought of. It is unlimited and infinite in potential. Your hidden resources can be tapped here. Connect with your unconscious mind through your feelings and intuition. Ideas from here come to you fast, like light bulb ideas. You don't have to think things through. It comes like fresh insights. It's that first idea or gut-feel you get. We sometimes dismiss the gut-feel with a 'let me think about it first'. It's best to trust your intuition, your gut-feel. It's more real than thoughts. Your inner-tuition is your inner wisdom, your inner guidance about what's right for you.

Your Higher Conscious Mind

Also called your Higher Self, your guiding spirit, the creator in you – the eternal you that goes beyond time and space. It's your most magnificent and perfect self. Your Higher Self sees you and your life as perfect and sees everyone else as perfect. It is beyond judgement, all-loving and all-forgiving. Your Higher Self is your fifth-dimensional aspect and can also be sixth, seventh and higher dimensional. It has your blueprint of perfect health which can be accessed for recreating good health. Your Higher Self is the source of manifestation and will always give you what you ask for, provided you have positive beliefs about it. For a close connection, your Higher Self wants you to be free from negative emotions and limiting beliefs. That's why the path of healing and transformation is the path of evolution – the path of becoming more of your Higher Self. Your Higher Self is all-powerful, yet humble. It can create anything you ask for and can uncreate anything you don't want, such as disease and unhappiness. It wants the best for you, yet respects free will and must be asked. That's why goals and intentions are important, as they activate higher assistance in achieving outcomes. All you have to do is ask. Asking is creating. This is not asking like a helpless child – 'please give me, please help me'. Asking means aligning yourself with your Higher Self, the creator in you and becoming a creator. It invokes the divine creative power.

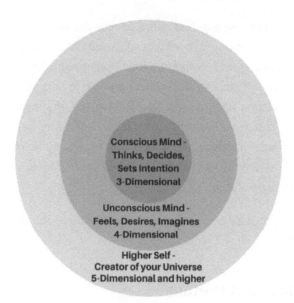

Figure 3: Your Three Minds

Creating in Synergy

Your Conscious Mind sets the creation process in motion with thought, intention, decision, clarity and focus. The Conscious Mind directs the Unconscious Mind with intention and visualisation. The Unconscious Mind is excited by the pictures, sounds and feelings and desires to set its creation process in motion. Your Higher Self is the source of manifestation and will always give you what you ask for, provided the path is clear and the message is delivered accurately. Here's the secret: The path of communication with the Higher Self is through the Unconscious Mind (see Figure 3). That's why visualisation and good feelings are so powerful. It's the language of the Unconscious Mind. The Unconscious Mind is very magical and also childlike. That's why we have to be very clear and specific about what we want, as if you explain it to a child. The more detailed, the better. State it with a positive focus towards what you want. The Conscious Mind sets the goal and decides what you want. The Unconscious Mind fetches the goal and works the magic in how to bring it about. Visualise only the desired end result. Leave the processes and steps to your Unconscious Mind. It is very imaginative and creative and knows best how to bring things about. The Unconscious Mind must also feel worthy of approaching the Higher Self. Release any negative emotions or limiting beliefs first to clear the path. The three minds work best in synergy. Knowing their unique functions allows you to work the Laws of Manifestation and Creation masterfully.

The ultimate aim is integration of the three minds into wholeness

Be Clear and Certain

It's important to be clear on your goal and intentions. Clarity and certainty is the energy you want to send out into the universe. If you are unsure, you send out an energy of uncertainty ahead of you. You then create more uncertainty and get wishy-washy results. As a powerful creator, make firm decisions with clarity, certainty and direction. This sends out a strong and firm determination into the universe. This is good leadership too. Leaders make decision. If you say: 'Mmmmm I'm not sure, what do you think?', others will make decisions for you and you end up giving more power to their opinions than your own inner-tuition. Take charge of your own life and your own destiny and be fully committed to what you do. When you say: 'This is what I believe we do, let's do it now', you radiate the certainty, clarity, direction and leadership people want and appreciate.

Be Aligned

Bring yourself into alignment with your Higher Self, the Universe and the source of creativity and light. Do this through intention and feelings of love, joy and gratitude. Then you know what you want to manifest will be in alignment with your purpose and in the highest and greatest good of all. The whole universe will support you and conspire to bring you what you ask for, and it will happen so much quicker. When in alignment, what you seek seeks you and wants to flow through you. Manifest from the heart from within a loving joyful vibration.

Be Open to Receive

Energy is electric and magnetic. When you envision your creation and send it out into the Universe, that's electric energy. Now, also indicate that you are willing and ready to receive, by bringing your vision into your heart, feeling positive, loving feeling for it. That's the magnetic energy completing creation by drawing your vision through into form. In this way, you are telling the Universe that you are ready and open to receive.

Master your Hologram

Newton's gravitational laws keep the concrete three-dimensional world of particles, the world of your Consciousness Mind, in good running order. We can rely on Newtonian science to build walls that keep roofs up and bridges that stay solid and strong. In the subtler realms of your subtle minds, the laws become more quantum physical, even holographic. Here everything is energy. Energy follows thought. Focus changes the waves of pure potential into particles, the building blocks of form. Quantum physicists have found that electrons only become particles when observed. When an electron is not observed, they become waves of energy again. Focused energy transforms nothing into something. Your universe is subjective in nature and moulds itself to the focused thoughts and energy you put into it. Reality is a construct of the mind, created with your thoughts.

Quantum scientists (Talbot, 1991) now believe that even the brain is holographic, with memory not localised in specific brain areas but rather distributed throughout the brain as a whole. This explains how the Unconscious Mind has the space to store all of your memory. It also explains how learned skills can be transferred from one part of the brain and body to another. Perlmutter and Villoldo (2011) describe how after stroke damage, people's brains can adapt by using alternative pathways to regain functionality such as speech or the use of a hand. MRI scans still show the damage in the related part of the brain, so the relearning is taken over by other parts of the brain.

All consciousness is interconnected. Swiss psychiatrist, Carl Jung, described this connection as the collective unconscious that is shared by all people. It explains phenomena like telepathy. Every thought and action affect the consciousness of the whole. This has tremendous implication for mastery and for impacting the world positively.

Your holographic universe is infinite in abundance and potential. Like a hologram, everything is interconnected, and every tiniest bit contains the design and essence of the whole. The quantum potential is a field that permeates all space. All particles are non-locally interconnected. Even when electrons are experimentally separated, they communicate and synchronise movement over vast distances, instantaneously. All things are part of an unbroken web communicating and moving in coordinated, organised unity, as is visible in the synchronicity of a school of fish moving as one, or a flock of birds flying in formation. Past, present and future all run concurrently, and everything is created in the present moment of now. Your goal or intention is the slide in the projector of your hologram. You create all your experiences in your universe. Is a holographic projection real? No, you can wave your hands through it and you can walk through it. It's an illusionary projection. Our perceived reality is an illusionary projection. If something in your universe is not quite the way you intended, you can change the slide in the projector and recreate your reality.

Modern quantum science is discovering what the ancient wisdom teachers knew. Old and new are so similarly described as is evident in the ancient Hawaiian philosophy of Huna:

Seven Principles of Huna: Ancient Wisdom

- The world is what you think it is (BE AWARE)
- There are no limits, everything is possible (BE FREE)
- Energy flows where attention goes (BE FOCUSED)
- Now is the moment of power (BE HERE)
- To love is to be happy (BE HAPPY)
- All power comes from within (BE CONFIDENT)
- Effectiveness is the measure of truth (BE POSITIVE)

Serge K. King (2008)

Mastery is stepping into your greatness

Powerful Intentions

Set intentions for everything you do. Set an intention for your day, your week, your month and the year ahead of you. Set intentions for every event, project and interaction you have. That sets the tone and creates your desired outcomes ahead of you. Linda, who has a demanding job as a nurse in a busy hospital, sets a simple intention for her working day before she sets off: 'Today I want to make somebody happy and grateful'. This regular, rewarding practice changes her outlook on her day as she creates and consequently enjoys many priceless moments of joyful interactions with colleagues and patients alike.

State your intention positively and in present tense, as if you already have it now. Keep it simple, clear and specific so that a five-year-old can understand it. Then you know your Unconscious Mind, your child mind, will be clear on what you want. Your Unconscious Mind lives in the present so bring your goal out of the future in the present. As an example, instead of saying 'I want to have a new job', say 'I see myself in a new job'. Bind in all your senses – I see, I hear, I feel ... 'I have a new job, I see myself doing ... in a pleasant environment' (describe in detail), 'I hear the sound of ...' (children laughing), 'I enjoy getting feedback from people saying ...', 'I feel good knowing I make a difference ...'

Your Unconscious Mind doesn't process negatives, so state your intention positively and towards what you want. As example, instead of saying 'I don't want to be nervous when I speak', say 'I speak with ease and comfort from the heart'. Instead of saying 'I don't want to disappoint people', say 'I enjoy bringing inspiration to people and seeing them smiling'.

Believe fully and your goal will be achieved. At the same time, let go of the importance of it. Detach from the outcome. Accept in good faith and trust that whatever happens will be for your highest and greatest good. That keeps the ego and its investments out of it. Eagerness and desperation constrict your energy and dispel the desired outcome. Stay open and trusting that everything will work out for the best. Be grateful in advance. Gratitude raises your vibrations and attracts more things to be grateful for.

Powerful Visualisations

Now that you are clear on what you want, and the specifics outlined, engage your unconscious mind, your emotional mind with a powerful visualisation of the end result. Visualise only the final outcome, the end result. Leave the how it's going to happen to your magical mind, your creative unconscious mind, that can bring things about in surprising ways.

Powerful visualisations activate mental pictures, sounds and feelings in ways that excite, motivate and mobilise your unconscious mind:

- What is the last thing that needs to happen for you to know you've achieved your goal?
- How will you know you've achieved it?
- What do you see?
- Where are you?
- Who else is there?
- What are they saying to you?
- What are you saying to yourself?
- What else do you hear?
- How good does it feel, having achieved this?

Now step into your picture, look through your own eyes.

- What do you see around you?
- Add some colour to make it even more compelling.
- If you make your picture brighter, clearer, bigger, bolder, would it be more compelling?
- Play with it, photoshop it.
- What do you hear?
- Turn up the volume and the clarity of the sound.
- What are you saying to yourself?
- What are others saying to you?
- Hear it clearly.
- What are you feeling?
- Really turn up the intensity of those feelings; enjoy feeling those good feelings.

Now, as good as it feels, step out of your picture.

- Look at yourself in your picture.
- How are you different now that you have achieved your goal?
- What are you wearing? What is the expression on your face?
- What's your posture? How do you stand, sit, walk, carry yourself?
- Put a frame around your picture.

Now that you are clear about your desired end result you can take your picture; your vision into the Masterful Manifestation meditation.

Meditation

Masterful Manifestation
(First release any fears or doubts using the Higher Self-Healing meditation of Step 2)

- Start by grounding yourself. Connect with your guides and ask for protection; to be held in the light. Set your intention for your meditation. Breathe to energise yourself. Through breathing, generate the energy it takes to create. Connect with your Higher Self and draw down the light into you. Expand your awareness wider, beyond the room, beyond this three-dimensional world of form into the worlds of pure energy and potential. Enter the quantum realm – your creation zone.
- See yourself in alignment with the entire universe – like planets coming into alignment. See yourself, your Higher Self, the sun, the moon, all the planets, the entire universe and the infinite Source, all coming into alignment. Visualise source energy being channelled in through your Crown. See yourself brightening up like a sun. Every cell in your body is being flooded with this light, pure creative force. House this light, this energy inside of you, so that you hold the equivalent of energy in your physical and energy bodies of what you want to manifest.
- Now ask for what you want, set your intention. Visualise what you want as a clear picture, feeling or sound – be specific, fill in the details, enjoy creating. Your picture with all the sounds, sights and good feelings is your creation. Place your intention, your creation, your picture like ripples

of information into the quantum field of pure electric creative energy.

- Now, draw it to you magnetically. By bringing it in, you are stating that you are open, receptive, in alignment and ready to receive. Bring it into your heart centre. This is symbolic of you receiving it and bringing yourself into alignment with what you want. Breathe life into your creation. Thought and breath imprints the aether. You enliven thought with breath. Feel loving, joyful emotions, the drive, enthusiasm, excitement and passion for what you want – the faith and trust in yourself and in the universe supporting you. Know that you've created in your moment of alignment. Now you can just let it go with gratitude. Let it be, in good faith and trust, it is done. From now on you can just enjoy taking inspired action as if you already have it now.

- With gratitude, acceptance and trust in the wisdom of the universe, bring yourself back to the world of form, staying expansive and knowing that at some level what you want already exists for you, and it's just a matter of no time at all, for it to follow you through into the world of form. Ground yourself back here, so through grounding you intend to anchor your creation into the world of form.

Visit
www.brightfuturenow.co.uk/meditations
to download or listen to a free audio meditation:
Masterful Manifestation Meditation

Step 4: Master the Laws of Love

Having established and fulfilled a healthy ego in Step 3, you have a strong foundation from where to transcend the ego, reach out to others in love and grow into higher consciousness beyond the self.

Journey Through the Chakras: Heart Chakra

Colour	Green
Location	Centre of chest, at the physical heart
Qualities and Functions of the Heart Chakra	Love – for self and others, compassion, forgiveness, kindness, goodwill, generosity, gratitude, light-heartedness, joy, balance and transcendence of ego. Love starts with self-love. Self-love is the foundation of good health and happiness; the foundation from where you can reach out to bring love to others. The Heart Chakra is linked to the hand chakras (minor chakras in the palms of your hands) through which you can reach out to touch, love and heal others. The heart centre opens through forgiveness. It is really love and forgiveness that raise your vibrations to transcend ego and live as your true Higher Self (see Table 1 above).
Key Functions for Mastery	• Coming into balance. • Becoming the wise observer and moving beyond projection. • Embracing love and compassion as opportunity for mastery. • Recreating your universe through forgiveness. • Mastering the Universal Laws of Love.

Love is divine power. Balance is completion. Forgiveness is the true work of mastery.

Master the Key Universal Laws of Love

- *The Law of The Present Moment*: By living in the moment, centring ourselves in love and being in service to others, we live in divine flow.
- *The Law of Unconditional Love*: Loving yourself and others unconditionally, is honouring yourself and others, respecting everyone's unique soul path. It is loving without judgement or reservation, with an awareness that we are all One. When we love without condition or restraint we connect in a profound manner with our own Higher Self. We notice that we say the right things at the right time in our communication with others while loving unconditionally. Life and events seem to flow to us in a more joyous and agreeable manner. Everything seems easy when living in unconditional love.
- *The Law of Compassion*: The Universe does not judge us, it only provides consequences, lessons and opportunities to balance and learn through the Law of Cause and Effect. Compassion is the recognition that we are each doing the best we can within the limits of our current beliefs and capacities. The more loving kindness and forgiveness you give to yourself, the more you can give to others.
- *The Law of Forgiveness*: Seeing everyone as connected and all as love. Forgiveness restores wholeness and brings peace.

Finding Balance

A key life lesson for many of us is finding balance. As I work and interact with people, it becomes progressively clearer that more and more people feel over-stretched and stressed with ever increasing work pressure and demands on their time. Their lives feel out of balance. What do we mean by finding balance? Some may think of 'the balancing act to get things done', or the 'balancing act of spinning all those plates' or 'work–life balance' or 'all in good balance'. However, it's more than that. Balance is really a matter of spiritual evolution. When we find the balance point of all our experiences (resisting nothing and chasing nothing) and integrate it by bringing ourselves into balance, we can finally ascend.

We are ultimately seeking balance. When we find it, the lessons of life are learnt, and we are free to be and create.

So how do we really find the balance point, the point of liberation and transformation into a new way of being?

Balancing Doing with Being

The classic yin yang balance; balancing action, activity and business with rest, recuperation, sleep and nurturing. This is where we often get things out of balance, work pressure and family responsibilities being the main culprits. All disease is imbalance. Your body can tell you when you get out of balance, by creating stiffness, aches and pains, often on one side more than the other, indicating a classic yin/yang imbalance in the body. We just have to tune in, feel and listen. All this doing needs to be balanced with just being – enjoying life. Meditation as a regular practice can be a trusted friend here. Meditation is a treat, not a chore – a practice of non-doing, of un-doing, of just being – a practice aimed at restoring balance.

Balancing Giving with Receiving

Why does it seem easier to give than to receive? Could you allow yourself to receive? Receiving without an 'Ah you shouldn't have …'. Receiving graciously with just a 'thank you', allowing others the pleasure of doing something for you. Balancing the give-and-take in relationships, between what's good for us personally and what's good for the needs of those people we care about, is an essential fine art and you owe it to yourself.

Balancing Others with Self

Many of us have been raised with the idea to put other people first. It's a misconception that is misunderstood and mis-practised. When you feel duty-bound to do more for others or want to please others at the expense of yourself, you can create energetic imbalances which can leave you feeling resentful and drained. No one is more important than anyone else. We are all equal in value. Caroline Myss (1996), in her discussion of healthy self-esteem, refers to two spiritual laws: 'honouring one another' and 'honour oneself'. These two laws are equal in importance and we are to balance how we practise and apply them. Through the practice of balance, we assert healthy boundaries.

Balancing Past and Future with the Present Moment

We create anxiety and stress through fear-based thoughts – regretting past events and thinking too far ahead, anticipating undesired future outcomes. When we come into the present moment, release takes place. Here nothing needs to be achieved or controlled. The present moment is completely free from stress. Here we can open up to the joy of life. The present moment is expansive, and time stands still. In the present, you can just be, flow and create.

Balancing Planning with Flowing

Planning serves its purpose. It's good to plan your day and scan your week ahead. Set your intentions and then let go of the importance of it. It's a strange paradox, yet it keeps any self-investment out of it. Set your aim and then flow with the river of life. As much as we may want to pursue our own agendas, and sometimes it's very important to do so, equally if we stay mindful of the bigger picture this can help us to find good balance. Flowing opens us up to our inner guidance and life's surprising synchronicities through which things fall in place in magical ways.

Balancing Head with Heart

Practically all inner conflict is a conflict between the head and heart; being in two minds about what to do and what's important to us. Too often we overthink things whilst dismissing that wise intuitive inner voice only to regret it later. Sounds familiar doesn't it? So, the ultimate balancing act is balancing the logical thinking head with the intuitive heart; the analytical conscious mind with the creative, emotional unconscious mind; the controlling ego self with the comfortable and ever expansive true self. This integration brings the minds into oneness, wholeness and peace. Then the minds can work together in synergy, harmony and balance. This is true healing; the healing that brings transformation and enlightenment.

Balancing Heaven with Earth

In the body, the lower chakras are more yin, feminine and earthly and are about our grounding, our connection with the Earth, our physical and emotional health. The higher chakras are more yang, masculine and heavenly; being about the mind, the higher mind and spirit. Regardless of our gender, we each have both yin and yang energies in us and our life lesson is to bring them into balance inside of us. The Heart Chakra is the midway point, the natural place of balance and harmony. The heart connects and unites heaven and earth in the body. The heart is the gateway. When we slip into this balance point and reside more in the heart, a gateway opens; a gateway to a more magical life where things flow and work out miraculously and you are liberated to evolve more into your expansive, magnificent and infinitely creative true self.

When we are in balance within ourselves we embody the knowledge of the universe, and we can expand beyond measure.

Advanced Healing Practices

The Healing Power of Relationships

In therapy, the topic of challenging relationships often comes under discussion. We grow and evolve through relationships – all relationships; those with partners, family, friends, colleagues and strangers alike. We are all on a path of healing. So what role do our relationships play in this healing process?

Mastering the Art of Relationships

Our relationships with others, mirror our primary relationship – with ourselves. Through relationships, we evolve and learn more about ourselves. To master the art of relationships, we have to deepen our understanding of the deep psychology of perceptions and how we project our own perceptions onto others.

The Psychology of Perceptions and Projections

Carl Jung, the psychologist, said that we project our deep-seated unconscious issues out onto people around us. We then think they are the problem, because we couldn't see it in ourselves. This is all part of the process of learning about ourselves. In the holographic model of the universe, there is no one outside of you, that isn't you. Taking responsibility for our own perceptions, takes self-empowerment and personal transformation to a whole new level of mastery. When we take charge of our perceptions we can change it at any time, for example, from 'People will think I'm crazy' to 'People find this inspiring', or 'She's an obsessive perfectionist' to 'She's so well organised and I can learn a lot from her'. When we challenge and change our perceptions (the slide in the hologram), everything and everyone around us changes, and quite magically, we project out changed characters and experiences in our universe.

Your Holographic Universe and Its Many Mirrors

What you see in others is who you are yourself – what you like and don't like. We are always looking in a mirror. You are the operator in the projector booth of your hologram. You put the slides (thoughts and perceptions) in your projector. These images are then projected out, creating your unique experiences in your holographic universe. When we are still unaware, our perceptions are projected unconsciously. The most powerful transformational work you can do is bringing your projected perceptions into consciousness awareness. If our views of reality are only a perception and everything we perceive outside of us is a projection from inside of us, then it's time to really take charge of our perceptions. It's so human to blame others and want them to change. Taking responsibility for your own perceptions and embarking on this great inner work is real empowerment, true mastery, and most rewarding, as the change you experience will be immediate and radical.

Mastery is living from the inside out

Perceptions are Projected

- We grow and evolve through relationships.
- Our view of others is only a perception.
- We tend to project our perceptions onto others.
- What you see in others is who you are yourself.
- We are always looking in a mirror.
- You are in charge of your perceptions and can challenge and change them.
- We can only change ourselves – we cannot change others.
- When you change your perceptions, people change, and your experiences too.
- Everyone around you is your teacher – helping you to learn something about yourself. That's how you grow and evolve. Your greatest teachers are those testing people around you.

Owning your Perceptions and Projections

To bring about such radical change in your universe, you first have to own your projections and take full responsibility for them being the result of your perceptions. It takes courage to own them and do the inner work of transformation. Our projections point to unhealed aspects in us. As example, if you experience a colleague or family member being overpowering, it can be very testing. It can make you feel angry and powerless. By owning the projection, you can feel inside and identify the unhealed aspect in you. It may be a limiting belief about your own abilities. Perhaps you withhold expressions, fearing people's opinions. It may be time to express yourself and take your power back. It may be time to step into your own true power.

Perceptions aren't truths. We simply make them up. Owning your perceptions, challenging and changing them, offers you the wisdom to grow and evolve.

Self-Mastery through Changing Perceptions

Once you've owned your projection, you can change your perceptions about yourself and the other person. In the *Ho'oponopono* practice, we thank the other person for the learning experience. As we forgive and cut connections, we cut away the old perceptions. Then you are free to see them in their true light and assert your own true light. All forgiveness is self-forgiveness through which you are integrating previously unhealed aspects of yourself into wholeness. Adopting new empowering beliefs is so much easier then. As example: 'As I own my own power, and express myself honestly, I can relate to others equally. As I step into my own power, I can empower others to do the same'. Beliefs and perceptions aren't real, yet they do create your reality. When you project a new truer version of yourself out into your universe, you create a new reality and people around you seem to change towards you instantly. Your universe becomes more peaceful and joyful, while you grow in insight, healing and mastery.

When the lessons are learned, the projections can stop. Instead of projecting, you can extend yourself and your work in the world.

The Healing Power of Forgiveness

Forgiveness is essential for your health. Research has shown how anger, resentment and hostility physically impacts on the heart as it can cause hardening of your arteries and heart attacks (Edwards, 2010).

True healing often involves deep forgiveness or a shift in consciousness; changing your perceptions of those testing people in your life, and those who caused you hurt. This is based on a recognition that, from a higher perspective, everything happens for learning and growth. Hypnotherapist, Robert Schwartz, describes these interactions from a pre-life planning perspective. He describes how soul groups co-plan and agree life events. How we pre-plan our growth experiences and it may include many individual agreements to meet and work with certain people in certain places at certain times. For you to learn the growth lesson you wanted to, others agreed to act out certain roles (Schwartz, 2012). Some of those roles may feel testing but ultimately, they are acts of love as it helps you to grow and evolve. Seeing it like this, certainly makes forgiveness easier. In essence, we ask for forgiveness that they had to act out those challenging roles for you to learn your lessons. Forgiveness is your most powerful mastery practice. Forgiveness retrieves your soul and liberates you from the past. All forgiveness is a gift of healing and self-renewal.

Everything happens for a reason and ultimately for your growth

Steve started his first job in a retail business. Only a few weeks into the job, he became disheartened. He really struggled to get on with the two business partners. He was left to figure a lot out for himself and he felt unsupported. Exacerbated, ready to leave, I took him through the *Ho'oponopono* process, explaining the magic of it. We worked to truly forgive and recreate his existing perceptions of the business partners. A week later, Steve said to me, 'I can't believe the change in my managers. It is as if they've undergone personality transplants. They can't do enough for me.' That's the kind of miraculous results you can create with the powerful process of *Ho'oponopono*.

***

Kath shares her experience of *Ho'oponopono*: 'I have had some amazing experiences with the *Ho'oponopono* meditation. So, I naturally fell back on this powerful practice after a family rift at my daughter's wedding that caused me a great deal of negative feelings towards my brother-in-law and sister-in-law, something which was constantly eating away at me. We were all invited to another family wedding, and after not seeing them for over a year, I was feeling a great deal of anguish. As soon as I practised the *Ho'oponopono* meditation, repeating the forgiveness mantra in my mind, they immediately apologised, and I told them I loved and forgave them. I felt great peace. We may not be best friends again, which is fine but the hurt and negativity have been healed, and when we do meet at family functions, we can interact, and I feel calm, confident and in control. *Ho'oponopono* is a truly positive and magical healing experience.'

***

Advanced Uses of *Ho'oponopono*

Possibly one of the most magical healing meditations, *Ho'oponopono*, the Huna forgiveness ritual, wipes the slate clean. If you've had a challenging experience in any of your relationships, *Ho'oponopono* facilitates forgiveness and allows you to change existing perceptions. Whatever your perception of another person may be, it's just a perception. Equally, how others perceive you, is only a perception. If you have done something to offend others (something that happens to all of us – mostly unintentionally), then the *Ho'oponopono* forgiveness process is the way to clear the air and put things right.

We can use this same powerful forgiveness meditation in more advanced ways – to change perceptions, clear the slate and recreate your world; your holographic universe afresh.

Healing Perceptions of Money, Business or your Home

Our relationships go beyond people. You can use *Ho'oponopono* to recreate your relationship, for example, with money, your business and your house. If your experience of money is limited rather than abundant, investigate your beliefs around money; whether you believe you deserve abundance. What's your relationship with your business, job or career? How would it be different if you could change your perception of it; if you believed in it; if you were grateful for it? How do you feel about your home? Even if you desire a change, it will come your way more easily from a basis of love and appreciation. Equally, if you're trying to sell your house and you are too attached to it, potential buyers won't get a feel for it. Sometimes we are attached to places where we have lived or visited, and we still have one foot in that place. As a result, we could feel scattered or 'all over the place'. This stops us from moving on, feeling rooted and being truly present. Letting go energetically allows you to feel whole again; brings movement and new opportunities into your life.

Self-Forgiveness

Do you have past experiences that continue to bring up feelings of anger, guilt or embarrassment? If so, these events are still unresolved in the mind and are keeping you attached to the past. It's time to clear the self-criticism, free yourself and bring love and compassion to your life. Change the inner critical voice to a compassionate voice.

Forgive any negative thoughts, images and perceptions that pop up in your mind. This can happen when the ego mind creates its concerns and unhelpful interpretations. Instead of struggling against them, simply forgive them. Forgiveness clears the screen and then you can recreate afresh.

Being at Peace

It's best for your own healing to be at peace with everyone in your life. You don't have to necessarily like everyone, and there will certainly be people you won't want to spend a lot of time with and that's alright. As long as you are at peace in your own heart for your own sake. Forgiveness restores your energy and your health and sets you free. This release can feel like a huge weight lifting as you put the past behind you peacefully.

The Mastermind-set

- We are all One.
- There is no one outside of me that isn't me.
- I'm in charge of my thoughts and perceptions; the slides that create my holographic universe.
- Through forgiveness I heal and set myself free.
- I welcome joy and peace into my life.
- I bring love and compassion to myself.

Mastery Practices

- Practise bringing joy into your life every day. It can be something simple like smelling a flower.
- Practise an inner smile; as if you smile inside. The corners of the mouth might curl upwards slightly as the inner smile brings instant upliftment. This practice is described in more detail in Step 10.
- Practise finding and maintaining balance in all things.
- Practise forgiveness of others, of yourself, your perceptions and any unhelpful thoughts.
- Move beyond projection, then you can extend yourself in the world.

Meditation

Ho'oponopono: Cutting Connections

An Exercise in Forgiveness, Healing and Peace-Making

This meditation serves as a true telepathic communication from within the collective mind – Higher Self to another's Higher Self. At this level, forgiveness comes easier. The result is miraculous as it clears the old energy and literally wipes the slate clean.

You choose who you want to cut with. When you do this meditation for the first time, it's best to cut with everyone to clear your energy of past connections. You can always reconnect again, and when you do, they experience you for who you are at present, free from the past. People's opinions of who you used to be can keep you back. Therefore, as you cut the connections, you can stand in your own true light and be seen for who you truly are. This process is based on your projected perception and is therefore a great way to manage and master your perceptions as well.

Results of the Ho'oponopono *Meditation*

- Healing: physical, emotional and spiritual.
- Forgiveness (totally forgive and forget): of self and others, leads to liberation and miraculous transition to a higher level of consciousness.
- Clean slate: an official new beginning.
- Energy retrieval: retrieving your energy and bringing it back into integrity.

Process

- Imagine you are in a place of no time and infinite space.
- Create a platform in your mind onto which you can invite people with whom you want to cut the energy cords.
- Start the healing process. Connect with source, with the light. See yourself in a ray of light; the infinite source of love and healing. Take this healing light into all of your being. See yourself becoming lighter and brighter. Feel the warmth and love of this healing light. Fill yourself up to overflow. Then channel this infinite source of love and healing to flow onto the platform, facilitating the healing of those you are going to call up.
- Keep flowing the infinite source of love and healing through you and onto the platform.
- Start by inviting people onto your platform. You can call them up in groups. These may be parents, grandparents, brothers, sisters, uncles, aunts, children, nephews, nieces, friends (old and new), colleagues, business clients, teachers, mentors, students, partners, ex-partners, neighbours or anyone brought up by your unconscious mind. You can call up versions of yourself, for example, your younger self, your angry self or your doubtful self. You can also call up your concept of money, your house, your job or business.
- You can have a discussion in your mind, individually or as a group, clearing any issues.
- Then say: I'm sorry, please forgive me. I love you. I thank you. Forgive any negative thoughts, and perceptions too. When the forgiveness is done, the energetic cords will dissolve, and they will float off the platform, becoming one with the light. Remember, they are your projections, so the forgiveness is really up to you. Besides, it's for your own healing. You will know it's done when inner peace and harmony returns. As the old energy cords dissolve, you are

retrieving your energy and your aspects back to you. Then you can see them in their own true light again, creating new positive perceptions. You can also be seen standing in your own true light, free from the past.

- When the platform is clear, it represents your clean slate, your official new beginning. This is the wonder of life: you can always start again. Every day can be a new beginning.
- As you forgive and let go, you become whole again. This is healing and ultimately you are your own healer.
- Ground back in the body.

Visit
www.brightfuturenow.co.uk/meditations
to download or listen to a free audio meditation:
Ho'oponopono: *Cutting Connections*

Step 5: Master Your Mind and Your Thoughts

Continuing to explore our creative power, in Step 5 we face the creative power of thoughts and the importance of disciplined mental focus so that you can express your higher truth and unique gifts in alignment with your higher purpose.

Journey Through the Chakras: Throat Chakra

Colour	Sky blue
Location	Throat, neck and shoulder area
Qualities and Functions of the Throat Chakra	This is the realm of the conscious mind; of conscious choice, thought, attitude and voice. The Throat Chakra is your centre of communication, truth, listening, and creative self-expression.
Key Functions for Mastery	• Mastering the secrets of success – clarity, focus, action and belief. • Mastering mindful awareness of the nature of your thoughts. • Mastering positive thought and speech. • Mastering authentic creative self-expression. • Living your life's purpose masterfully. • Aligning what you want with your higher purpose.

The mind is fertile ground. Every thought is creation. There are no limits. Everything is possible.

Master the Key Universal Laws of Mind and Thought

- *The Law of Expectation*: Energy follows thought. What we assume, expect or believe colour and create our experience. You get what you expect. By changing our expectations, we change our experience of every aspect of our life. Ultimately and paradoxically, releasing expectations aligns you with your higher guidance and true purpose.

- *The Law of Choice*: The most basic choice we have in life is whether to expand or contract, whether to bring our creative and expressive energies out into the world in positive or negative ways. No matter what our circumstances, we have the power to choose our directions (Millman, 1993).

- *The Law of Discipline*: Discipline is the surest means to greater freedom and independence; it provides the focus to achieve the skill level and depth of knowledge that translates into more options in life. Meditation is a discipline (Millman, 1993).

- *The Law of the Present Moment*: Time doesn't exist. What we refer to as past and future have no reality except in our own mental constructs. The idea of Time is a convention of thought and language, a social agreement. In truth, we only have the Present Moment

- *The Law of Time*: The only moment we have is now. This is where we create. What we have done, is done. The future only happens in and from the present tense and is built of today's thoughts, dressed by emotions and driven by action (Millman, 1993).

- *The Law of Vibration*: This is the basis of manifestation. Nothing rests; everything moves; everything vibrates. This is the law of progress, of movement and of rotation.
- *The Law of Higher Will*: Surrendering your ego will to the guidance of a higher will and dedicating your actions for the highest good of all concerned, brings joy and meaning to your life.
- *The Law of Faith*: Faith is trusting that whatever is for the greatest good, will come about. Faith makes all things possible. Faith is following your intuition and holding your vision with conviction. Faith banishes fear and empowers choice to act and create.

Mastering Your Mindset

The mind is so powerful, and thoughts create outcomes, so when you take charge of your mind and bring mastery to your thoughts, you restore your health and bring balance to your life.

Does the Busy, Anxious, Analytical Mind Serve Any Purpose?

Our minds really reflect the nature of our busy lives and our mental approach to it. If your life is hectic and stressful, your mind will race with random, worrying thoughts. If you still have doubts about yourself, your ability to deal with things and concerns about what people may be thinking, then these worrying thoughts could develop into anxious thoughts.

The cause of stressful anxious thoughts run deeper still. The real reason has to do with awareness. When your awareness remains on the surface of the three-dimensional everyday busy life, the mind stays occupied with restless thoughts. An untrained mind runs a stream of senseless thoughts serving no particular purpose. There is so much more to your life than the three-dimensional narrow focus. That's only the tip of the iceberg of who you are.

Look After Your Nervous System

Give the nervous system a break from all the continuous stimulation. Spend time on your own, in nature and in stillness. Restore the balance by giving yourself time to rest and recuperate. Enjoy a creative activity such as gardening, cooking or music. Create calm by slowing your pace and be present in the moment. Calm doesn't come from some change in the external world. It has to be cultivated from within. When you do, you can engage your nervous system for what it was intended – creativity. Your nervous system is designed to bring about what you think about. Embrace your creative energy by channelling it constructively and positively into enjoyable projects. Align yourself with your destiny and set big intentions that drive and fulfil the vision of your more expansive multi-dimensional self.

In *Power up your Brain, the Neuroscience of Enlightenment* (Perlmutter and Villoldo, 2011), the evolution of the human brain is described, from the old reptilian brain (fight and flight) to the limbic brain (emotions), the neocortex (speech, writing and thinking) to the prefrontal cortex (the higher mind of creativity and initiative). Even though the old brain is still there in us, reacting with fear, greed, conflict and intolerance, human society is standing on the brink of an extraordinary leap in consciousness, they say. We are evolving in wisdom and higher awareness of connectivity, community, well-being, love, joy and enlightenment.

Rewire Your Brain

Due to our past experiences, the mind created neural pathways that keep triggering the same emotional reactions and limiting beliefs. In each new situation we have a choice whether to mull over anxious thoughts and reinforce the old reactive neural pathway, or to open up to new opportunities and new approaches, developing new positive emotions and beliefs. When we do, we create new neural pathways and rewire the brain. It's all about which thoughts we feed – fear or love.

***

There is a story of an old Cherokee teaching his grandson about life. 'A fight is going on inside me', he said to the boy. 'It is a fight between two wolves. One is evil – he reacts with anger, envy, sorrow, regret, greed, arrogance, self-pity, guilt, resentment, inferiority, lies, false pride, superiority, and ego', he continued, 'the other is good – he experiences joy, peace, love, hope, serenity, humility, kindness, benevolence, empathy, generosity, truth, compassion, and faith. The same fight is going on inside you – and inside every other person, too.'

The grandson thought about it for a while and then asked his grandfather, 'Which wolf will win?' The old Cherokee simply replied, 'The one you feed.'

***

So, with focused attention, you can change your thoughts and create new neural pathways. This investment changes your activities and your behaviour to bring about a positive change in your life.

Synergy of Minds

Because the Conscious Mind is only the tip of the iceberg, limited and slow, and the subtle minds below the surface are so infinite and expansive, it's easy to wonder if the Conscious Mind, with its senseless stream of busy thoughts, serves any purpose. Yet, the Conscious Mind starts the creation process and brings the essential functions of choice, decision, focus and direction to the process. Every aspect of the brain and mind serves an important purpose. It's best that the brain works in synergy as described in Step 3. Synergy means the whole is greater than the sum of its parts. Synergy of whole brain function can be achieved through relaxation, creativity, imagination and meditation. A calm mind is more expansive and enables clear perception. We have a choice, to feed the wolf of chaos, confusion, negativity, doubts and conflict, or the wolf of inner peace, love, joy, creativity and the gifts of your higher mind.

What Do Successful People Have in Common?

Neurolinguistic Programming, a science of excellence, success and the mind, found that people who achieve success, generally have these key practices in common:

- *Clarity*: they are clear on what specifically they want.
- *Focused intention*: they set clear intentions and keep a positive focus.
- *Disciplined thought*: they focus on what they want, not what they don't want. They may note their fears and focus on their desired results.
- *Action*: they take inspired action.
- *Belief*: they maintain positive belief.

The Creative Power of Your Mind

Your mind is immensely creative, and the possibilities are infinite. Your nervous system is designed to give you what you focus on. Everything starts with a thought, an idea that we energise through focus. What you focus your mind on is a conscious choice. What you focus on, you energise, expand, make more of. Focused thought expands the probability; the likeliness of the outcome.

An untrained, fearful mind creates 'what if' type of thoughts that energise exactly what we don't want and fear might happen. If you focus on what can go wrong, you create more fear. We seem to be good at telling ourselves what we don't want to happen. That leaves the Unconscious Mind confused about what you do want. Goals and intention give the Unconscious Mind a positive focus and direct the mind towards what you do want. Take note of what you don't want and focus on what you want. As example, 'I don't want to be late', is focusing on what you don't want. What do you want? 'I want to get there in time for a cup of tea before we start the meeting.' Equally, 'I don't want to be ill.' What do you want? 'I want to be healthy and well.' Better still, 'I am healthy and well.' Mental discipline turns the thoughts focused towards what you want. Your Unconscious Mind picks up on every thought, the suggestions (health or illness) hidden in your thoughts and the emotional vibration underlying it (fear of love). Your Unconscious Mind wants to please you and give you what you ask for, so be very specific, clear and positive in your statements.

Thought Awareness

Certain modes of thinking can drive negative emotional states:

- 'Should' and 'must' type thoughts as well as 'why don't they...' place high expectations on ourselves or others and are frustration drivers.
- 'Always' and 'never' type thinking pushes us into the extreme ('I am always helping you and you never help me') and are anger drivers.
- Catastrophising ('what if' type thoughts or beliefs that something is, or could be, far worse than it actually is) creates anxiety.
- 'All or nothing' or 'black and white' or 'right or wrong' or 'nobody' and 'everybody' type thoughts – absolutes rather than shades of grey – (nobody cares) are depression drivers.

Sometimes these thoughts are habitual thoughts that perpetuate the disempowering victim state. Bring the nature of your thoughts into your awareness. Are they helpful or harmful? Let your thoughts be kind, compassionate and reassuring to yourself as if you are your own best friend. Have faith in your intuitive guidance and trust that everything happens for a reason.

As You Think and Speak, So You Create

We create through thought, word and deed. The architect refines a concept of a house with a detailed plan, making it real. Equally, your goal written down refines your abstract thoughts or big picture vision and draws it through from the ideas plane into the three-dimensional world of form. Choice is very empowering. You always have more choices than you may believe at the time. At the level of the ego, as we chase our dreams, we assert our own will and exercise choice. The power of choice comes with the responsibility for consequences. At a more mature level, we seek meaning and purpose and endeavour to align our actions accordingly. As Caroline Myss (1996) says: 'Every one of us has an awareness that we were born for a specific purpose, that life contains a divine plan. The fifth chakra is the centre of that awareness.' This awareness of purpose is a strong motivating driver. The practice at the level of the Throat Chakra, is to surrender our personal will to a higher will, knowing our life has a divine plan. As you bring your goals and intentions into alignment with a higher purpose and calling, your life begins to feel fulfilling.

Sometimes we withhold expression thinking 'What will people think?' Expression exposes your world views, beliefs and perceptions. You may feel called to write a book or teach or paint or sing or offer alternative services such as energy healing. This can cause concerns about opinions or criticism or self-doubt as you put yourself out there. I experienced this when I published my first book. I then got to know the challenge and importance of expressing your own truth authentically. Withholding expression can cause throat-related health issues such as thyroid problems. Finding ways of expressing your own uniqueness creatively, is essential for your health and happiness. Opinions are just opinions, they aren't truths. Only you know what's right for you, and you know it through your inner compass.

You have infinite potential inside of you and the gifts to express it in your own unique way. You know more because you are more. You have an inner wisdom and a wealth of resources to tap. Creative expression is your birth right. You feel the calling and have those gifts for a reason. Someone will benefit from it.

Mindfulness

To practise more positive thinking patterns, continuously bring the nature of your thoughts into your awareness. By cultivating mindfulness, you can acknowledge and identify your existing thinking patterns. Thoughts can be habitual. Mindfulness creates a distance between yourself and your thoughts, allowing you to view yourself as separate from them. Incorporate mindfulness into your meditative practice and also into your moment-to-moment everyday life. Conscious awareness is the catalyst for change and mastery. Through mindfulness you can reflect on:

- *Your Perceptions*: Our reality is just a perception coloured in by our beliefs, values, memories and experiences. We always perceive subjectively. What am I not seeing?
- *Your Beliefs*: As self-fulfilling prophesies, our beliefs create our realities. Do I believe I can do it?
- *Your Thoughts*: Be mindful of your self-talk. As you think, so you create. Are my thoughts helpful to me?
- *The Mind-Body Link*: Mind and body is one interconnected whole. Pain and emotions are messages from your unconscious mind. Unresolved suppressed emotions can cause disease in the body. What are my body and my feelings telling me?
- *Your Responsibility*: Am I taking full responsibility for everything happening in my life?
- *Cause and Effect*: Embrace your creative energy. Am I acting or reacting? Am I a victim or a creator? What am I creating?

The master knows that what we think truly affects everyone

Cultivate a Compassionate Inner Voice

As you practise mastery, it will be natural to want to continue bettering yourself. Do so with compassion to yourself. An inner critical voice won't make you feel good about yourself and has the opposite effect. Replace the critical voice with a compassionate voice that still wants you to grow, yet nudges you gently in a non-judgemental compassionate way.

***

Josephine shares her experience of searching for inner peace and joy.

I have spent many years reading spiritual books, attending workshops, looking for the common threads that run through the main religions of the world, including paganism and shamanism. These threads enabled me to find my own spiritual truth, inner freedom, ability to control my own 'monkey mind' and find inner peace and joy.

I found inspiration in Viktor E. Frankl's book, *Man's Search for Meaning* ([1946] 2013) – a real tribute to hope. Viktor, who lived during the Holocaust, found that man can be stripped of everything and still find meaning in his life. I found further inspiration from *The Book of Joy* (2016), written by the 14th Dalai Lama and Desmond Tutu – the shared wisdom of two men who have had challenging experiences, yet are incredibly joyous. The Dalai Lama has been exiled from his home in Tibet and the archbishop witnessed the racial conflict during apartheid in South Africa.

The insight that I have taken from these three great men is that we are in control of our thinking. This choice determines the attitudes we adopt and our choice of reactions to life's events.

We choose the type of 'wallpaper in which to paper our minds'.

Reflections from Josephine Ormerod

***

The Mastermind-set

- Every thought is creation.
- There are no limits.
- Everything is possible.
- I am true to myself.
- I align my actions with my life's purpose and express it creatively and masterfully.

- Everything is energy and vibration.

Mastery Practices

- Incorporate healing sounds into your energy work or meditations:
    - HAW (a drawn-out haaawww) sound is earthy and good for grounding.
    - EEE (drawn-out eeeeee) sound clears the solar plexus and spaces.
    - AHH (drawn-out aaaaa) sound expands the heart, aligns you with the divine and speeds up manifestation.
    - HO (a throat-clearing) sound clears and energises the throat.
    - OHM (oooooohmmmm) sound is magnetic, drawing to you what you want to manifest
    - IAO (eeeeeeaaaaaaaoooooo) is the sound of the universe and connects you with spirit.

    Musician Tim Wheater, cured his own paralysing health condition through chants and now teach about the deep healing effects of sound on mind, body and soul.
- Thought awareness:
    - bringing your unconscious feelings, beliefs and perceptions into conscious awareness.
- Mindfulness and present moment awareness.
- Express yourself openly, honestly and lovingly.
- Align yourself with Spirit to create for the highest and greatest good of yourself, others and the planet.
- Surrender personal will to higher will.

Mastery is living in the now

Meditation

- Use the sound of mantras like *Ohm* to quiet the mind.
- Set intentions for your day, week or month ahead of you.
- Practise mindfulness of your thoughts, feelings, perceptions, beliefs and their creative power.

Mindfulness Meditation

- Sit upright, spine comfortably straight, and relaxed. Rest hands gently on your lap.
- Ground, connect and intend protection by placing yourself in the light.
- Set your intention for the meditation: to be with your own experience and bring awareness to thoughts, feelings, beliefs and perceptions.
- Now, bring your attention to your breathing, observing the natural rhythm of your breath.
- No need to change the breathing in any way, just observe it like a curious discoverer.
- Just paying attention to it, not thinking about the breath, being aware of it, feeling the sensation of it.
- Allow the breath to take centre stage in your awareness, just experiencing it.
- Notice the sensation of the cool air in the nostrils as you breathe in and the warmer sensation as you breathe out.
- Notice the little summersault of a turning point between the in-breath and the out-breath in the tip of the nostrils. Notice the gap between the in-breath and the out-breath.
- There is no right or wrong way of breathing, just your way, observing curiously.
- Bring a quality of kindness to your awareness – compassion, patience with yourself and your own experience, moment by moment.

- Use the breath like an anchor to reconnect to the here and the now.
- Thoughts and feelings may come and go. Just notice the thoughts – not judging them – just observing with curiosity and awareness.
- What images or feelings arise with the thoughts? People or events may pop up in your mind. What are your perceptions attached to these people and/or events?
- Anything that comes up, own it, give it attention, sit with it and learn from it.
- By staying mindful of our thoughts and feelings we are starting to let go of our habitual reactions.
- Paying attention to the nature of our thoughts and feelings is something we don't often do. By doing so, we bring the conscious and unconscious mind into union.
- As you sit with it, does the feeling change, perhaps into another feeling?
- Are the thoughts and perceptions attached to the feeling changing as well?
- Acknowledge these feelings as messages, learn from them with compassion in your heart, without judging or avoiding them.
- Learn in an effortless, reflective way. Then let it go. Release any concern about opinions too. Releasing brings joy.
- When the darkness goes the light sets in. Rest in the light. This is enlightenment that brings clarity. Be open and receptive to positive thoughts and feelings rising. These may be relief, lightness, calm, peace, care, kindness, love, self-love, joy and healing.
- Take this reflective, mindful practice into your everyday existence, regularly shining the light of awareness and transformation on your thoughts, beliefs and perceptions.

Adapted from sources: Rick Hanson (2009), Jack Kornfield (2002) and Dr J. Heaversedge and E. Halliwell (2010).

Visit
www.brightfuturenow.co.uk/meditations
to download or listen to a free audio mediation:
Mindfulness Meditation

Step 6: Master Refined Intuitive Perception

In Step 5 we explored the creative nature of thoughts and how you can turn your thoughts positive. At the level of the sixth chakra, the Third Eye, we want to take thoughts to another level of pure thought to cultivate inner peace, inner guidance and clarity.

Journey Through the Chakras: The Third Eye Chakra

Colour	Indigo
Location	The centre of your forehead
Qualities and Functions of the Third Eye Chakra	The Third Eye Chakra links to the higher mind functions of insight, intuition, visualisation, imagination, symbolic sight, higher vision and wisdom. The Third Eye is associated with your sixth sense, your psychic perception of clairvoyance. Clairvoyance is seeing clearly – not with the eye but with the soul – seeing beyond the physical world; seeing through the illusion; perceiving the truth. The Third Eye Chakra is about our true paths; about service to others. Here we ask the question: What am I doing here? We tune into our inner intuitive guidance for the answers. The Third Eye Chakra takes us from the personal higher mind to the impersonal higher mind. Detachment from subjective feelings and perceptions helps to see the higher truth. The Third Eye Chakra promotes awakening, consciousness and expanded awareness.
Key Functions for Mastery	• Mastering the Laws of Attention, Intention and Flow. • Mastering the art of visualisation as a primary tool for creation. • Mastering attuning to your inner-tuition.

Master the Key Universal Laws of Inner Knowing

- *The Laws of Creation*
  - *The Laws of Attention*: Energy follows thought. Whatever you focus on expands.
  - *The Law of Intention*: Intention releases a universal force that makes things happen.
- *The Law of Intuition*: We can only get in touch with our own source of intuition and wisdom when we no longer depend upon others' opinions for our sense of identity or worth. Do we value and trust our own intuition, or do we value and transfer authority to the opinions of others over our own inner feelings? Our intuition becomes more profound when we claim our own sacred identity.
- *The Law of Telepathy*: The will, projected from the point between the eyebrows, is known as the broadcasting apparatus of thought. When the feeling is calmly concentrated on the heart, it acts as a mental radio, and can receive the messages of others from far or near. In telepathy the fine vibrations of thoughts in one person's mind are transmitted through the subtle vibrations of astral ether and then through the grosser earthly ether, creating electrical waves which, in turn, translate themselves into thought waves in the mind of another person.
- *The Law of Divine Flow*: By living in the moment, centring ourselves in love and being in service to others (as opposed to service to self), we live in the law of divine flow. We stay in the moment by moment flow of our higher self, allowing and acting from love. When we are able to do this, we notice how we say just the right things, do what is best for all.
- *The Law of Faith*: Trust your own deepest intuition and wisdom as the final arbiter and source of your decisions.

Cultivate the New Mindset

The path of evolution is one of healing. We have to first heal the emotional mind, make peace with the past, release doubts and limiting beliefs and create a state of brain synergy. Then the gifts of the prefrontal cortex will be activated naturally – the gifts of your true state of joy, good health, youthfulness, love, creativity, wisdom, intuition, inspiration, insight and clear perception.

Pure Consciousness Is Without Thought

Peace and quiet, which most people long for, is just the threshold to the deepest state of awareness, which we can call pure consciousness. Here you can find the actual answer to the restless mind. Pure consciousness is without thought. It is the ground state of the mind; here you discover that awareness can rest in its own nature, without regard to any thoughts. Once you experience pure consciousness through meditation, your attention wants to go back there as often as it can.

This is not a passing desire. Experiencing pure consciousness brings you into contact with your quiet, peaceful source. Within a few days or a week of meditation, the entire body-mind begins to shift. This can be measured in terms of lowered stress hormone levels, lower blood pressure, and other biological markers. Just as important is how you relate to your mind. Most people mistake the activity in their minds – the constant stream of sensations, images, feelings, and thoughts – for the mind itself (The Chopra Centre, www.chopra.com).

The Pineal Gland: Key to Opening Your Third Eye

The Third Eye Chakra is linked to the pineal gland, a small light-sensitive gland in the centre of the head, believed by Descartes to be the seat of the soul. The pineal gland produces melatonin – a hormone that helps to regulate biological rhythms such as sleep and wake cycles. Melatonin is significant for its effects on our mood, immune function, circadian rhythms, and the quality and quantity of our sleep. Melatonin is known as an anti-ageing and anti-stress agent because it both suppresses cortisol and is a powerful antioxidant. The pineal gland produces serotonin and other consciousness enhancing neurochemicals, including pinoline and DMT (Dimethyltryptamine). These neurochemicals connect the mind and body (Chia and Thom, 2016). The pineal gland has a tranquillising effect on the nervous system. DMT, a plant-derived chemical found in the psychedelic Amazon brew, ayahuasca, is also said to be manufactured by the human brain. DMT is produced in the pineal gland during deep meditation and dream state. It alters our dream consciousness when it is released into the bloodstream during the Rapid Eye Movement (REM) phase of sleep. Dr Rick Strassman (2000) calls DMT the 'Spirit Molecule'. His life-long work is controversial, yet in his experimentation, volunteers consistently produced mystical experiences.

The pineal gland has to be healthy and activated for the third eye to open. The pineal gland can get calcified with time. Environmental toxins and dietary factors can play a role too. Increasing food types in the diet that are high in antioxidants, drinking pure water, getting sun exposure, doing yoga, breathing exercises and meditation all contribute to a healthy pineal gland. Most food sources list super-greens like broccoli, spirulina, wheatgrass, seaweed and green tea extract as essential brain food. Also, superfoods like turmeric, oregano oil, raw apple cider vinegar, tamarind, cacao, beets, organic olive oil, coconut oil, omega-3-rich nuts and seeds are powerful brain nutrients and cleansers. Perlmutter and Villoldo (2011) offer a detailed and a well-researched food and lifestyle regime that they say feeds the higher brain. According to the authors, the higher brain, the prefrontal cortex, is key to higher levels of consciousness and enlightenment, and has to be awakened. We can assist the process with the right nutrition, exercise, brain synergy and meditation.

Tuning into Your Inner-Tuition

The Third Eye Chakra promotes the practice of going within, mostly in meditation, yet also as you go through life following your inner radar moment to moment. The universe communicates all the time. All we have to do is be open, feel, listen and look for the signs and symbols that are in and around us. Unfazed by opinions and expectations, the master remains true to his internal frame of reference. Yes, spirit sometimes works through other people and helpful guidance can come that way. Always weigh it up against your own intuitive feelings. What's true for others, may not be true for you.

Silence is key to tuning into your intuition. In silence, inspiration can bubble up through the unconscious and penetrate into the conscious. Creative activity also opens us up to the still voice within. Intuitive guidance ultimately comes from your Higher Self, yet it follows the pathway through the Unconscious Mind. It can be heard like a subtle voice or seen as images. It can be felt like a gut-feel or an inner knowing. Such guidance comes to you in a snap out of nowhere. Be open to receive and trust what you get. The more you tune in, the more in tune you get with your inner-tuition. The truth can only be found within. Because you are a part in the universal hologram, what's in the whole is perfectly reflected in you. You have everything inside of you and the infinite wisdom of the whole can be accessed in you.

Mastery is going within

***

Geoff shares his reflections on mystical experiences: The human brain is logically structured. Desire and love come not from the brain, but from spirit. When in silence with the brain switched off, you can allow your desire and love to flow. Then the sky is the limit. When you know this, you don't have to work to get it, you already have it, and that inner knowing and seeing causes it to come into life. It's not the ego or self that is the difficulty, it's actually the brain that is trained to control. If a person says 'I never get any experiences' then the brain blocks it. When a person says and feels differently then the brain can't block it. So, what one feels and senses deeply within, is the art of all experience. We do not create what we want, that is brain function, we create what is possible.

The best tool you can use is SILENCE. In silence, the subtle realm of spirit penetrates your intuition, and wisdom surfaces.

Reflections from Geoff Owen

***

Visualisation: Seeing Clearly

The Third Eye Chakra is the centre of light and vision, and of your creative tools of imagination and visualisation that we described in-depth in Step 3. As you start the creation process with imagining and visualising, the images in your minds are a form of precognition. You see a vivid image of, for example, a new house, job or car in your mind first before it takes form. Through development of visualisation and imagination we simultaneously develop the means for clairvoyance (Judith, 2004). Clairvoyance is calling up relevant information from the hologram or akasha with a specific question which acts like a reference beam, lighting up specific information in the hologram. Regular practice will grow your confidence in your own innate clairvoyance. A clear and quiet mind receives the information more easily. Visualising or imagining the subtleties of energy, of yours or another's aura, is a powerful healing technique as we've practised in Step 1 and will do again in more depth in Step 8.

Cultivating your Psychic Perception

With practice we can activate and cultivate the psychic ability that is within us all. This is an innate gift and within all of our grasps. How can you practically enhance your psychic perception?

Expand Your Awareness

Learning the calm presence of being completely in the moment and fully in your senses, you experience a heightened state of awareness. Absorbing your surroundings in a single glance, can show you subtle, minute details about the situation and people around you that would otherwise have been outside of your awareness.

This awareness is not only visual but applies to all of your senses. You will be able to hear what people mean to say instead of what they are actually saying. Imagine walking into a room and instantly being aware of the entire situation and even the subtleties of the atmosphere and vibe in the room. All because of your heightened sense awareness.

How do you cultivate this ability? There are a few essential precursors to open up to your finer perception.

Stop Worrying

Worry and fear causes you to think about the past or future, instead of observing what is happening right in front of you. Mostly people are so busy, stressed and distracted that they are not fully present in their senses. When you are free from worries and fears, you can experience the world and events more clearly for what they are.

Clear Your Mind of Thoughts

When your mind is clear and at peace, you are free from distractions and any preconceived ideas. Then you can be present and able to accurately observe what is going on around you. Let the information come to you effortlessly and you'll be able to respond appropriately.

Focus on the Present Moment

Being fully present with all of your senses is the most powerful way to perceive reality. Reading people and situations accurately will become second nature as you learn to focus on what is happening right now.

One of the best ways of learning to focus only on the present moment is through meditation.

Peripheral Awareness

There is another technique you can use no matter where you are that can begin to fine-tune your perception and dramatically change your level of awareness. Peripheral Vision is a way of practising expanded awareness. In *Lifting the Veils of Illusion*, Peripheral Vision was described as an effective way of overcoming stress and relaxing the mind. There is more to this powerful practice. Your peripheral awareness is the key to psychic awareness, to sensing energy, perceiving subtleties and seeing through the veils. It's worth practising it and getting really good at it. Use the Peripheral Vision meditation below to familiarise yourself with the process and anchor in the practice so that you can use it effortlessly wherever you are.

Practise peripheral vision when you are waiting in a queue or sitting in a meeting or entering a room. Focus on one spot and then expand your awareness to take in the whole room. Your thoughts will slow down and turn off.

After that you can begin to observe clearly. Look around the room and take everything in through all your senses. What do you see, what do you hear, smell, feel, and taste? It is through sharpening your five senses that you will be able to open up to your sixth sense of intuition, energy sensations and psychic perception.

The Mastermind-set

- As I see it and believe it, I create it. I am always creating.
- I live consciously in the present moment, mindful of my surroundings, feelings and intuitions.
- As I flow with life and my inner guidance, I align with spirit and live my purpose.

- I see through the illusion of the three-dimensional world and view all situations with detachment, seeking symbolic meaning, wisdom and insight.

Mastery Practices

- Bring synchronicity and symbolic sight into your awareness.
- Have faith in your higher guidance and trust that everything happens for a reason.
- Keep a dream journal to analyse the symbolism of your dreams.
- Practise silence. Be still to tune into subtle sounds and listen intuitively.
- Create through visualisation.
- Let go – of control, blame, fears, judgements, external opinions and the need for proof.
- Practise detachment.
- Attune to your inner-tuition.
- Practise telepathy:
  - Telepathy, sending and receiving thoughts through the aether, the connective field of vibration, is a gift of the higher mind well worth practising and refining. We have all experienced thinking of someone and then they phone you. You may also have experienced sensing someone further away is in need of help. Telepathy is normal and easy when the mind is still and receptive to the subtle realm of vibration and connectivity. Consciousness is more symbolic than verbal, so messages from spirit come to you telepathically as well. Such messages appear, for example, in meditation as clear and instant guidance. While verbal messages can be interpreted, rightly or wrongly, symbolic messages are clear and certain. During an energy healing session, you and

your client's energy fields are connected, making it easy to tune into their thoughts and feelings. Be open to sending and receiving communication telepathically through your connection in the one universal mind that transcends time and space.

- Practise seeing auras:
  - Find a willing subject who's happy to be stared at for a while. Look at the person by focusing not on their eyes, but on the centre of their forehead; the area of their third eye. Soften your gaze and activate your peripheral vision (described below). Now, look through the person as if you want to look behind him. As you do, the white glow of the etheric body will jump out. If you look at it, it will disappear. So, keep your vision softened and bring it into your subtle peripheral awareness. Keep practising, it is really easy and you'll get better at it with practice.

Meditation

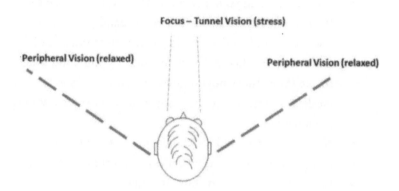

Figure 4: Peripheral Vision

Expanded Awareness by Activating Peripheral Vision

Peripheral Vision induces the parasympathetic nervous system. It puts you in a relaxed, creative and resourceful state. It is also a great learning state as the unconscious mind soaks up everything. In this state, the thoughts disappear and the mind clears. It's a state of heightened awareness; the secret to subtle perception – perceiving through the veils.

- Pick a spot on the wall in the middle of your vision and slightly above eye level. As you focus on that spot, begin to pay attention to the peripheral part of your vision.
- Soften the gaze and relax the jaw.
- Take the in-breath into the diaphragm and make the out-breath twice as long. A longer out-breath tells the body it's time to relax.
- With the eyes fixed on the one spot, bring into your awareness everything else around that one spot.

- Expand your awareness off into the periphery.
- Notice how much you can take in and become aware of in your peripheral vision (walls, floor, ceiling, items in the room).
- Can you expand your awareness 180°? What do you see in the corners of your eyes? Can you expand your awareness 360° all around you? What do you feel, hear and sense?
- It starts to feel like a daydream state, as you enter a light trance state. That's how we drive when we're in automatic mode. It's a safe way to drive as you are aware of everything around you.
- Notice how the mind has shifted into a relaxed state.

You can also practise peripheral awareness with your eyes closed:

- Bring your attention to your breathing.
- Continue the one-to-two-ratio breathing (deeper in-breath and longer out-breath).
- Now, much in the same way as we have done with the spot on the wall, focus on a spot of light, colour or an imagined spot in the centre of your inner vision.
- Allow your awareness to expand off to the left and the right of your inner peripheral vision simultaneously.
- Wider and wider; as if you ask yourself: 'What is there in the far left and the far right of my inner vision?'
- Yes, it is nothing; the great nothingness; the void.
- Take yourself off into the void; enter the void; the quantum field of energy.
- You may feel like you become one with the void.
- This is a state of infinite creativity, potential and resources.
- You can uncreate any unwanted thought or issue by taking it into the void.
- Watch it disappear into the void; let it go.
- From the void; the infinite pool of potential, you can also draw any resources that you feel you want to activate, for example, confidence, strength, trust, self-belief, etc.

- When you bring yourself back, do so with the intention of staying in this expanded state of awareness, alert and refreshed and yet relaxed and creative.
- Become more centred and grounded. Open your eyes and re-energise by taking a few deep breaths.

Practise Peripheral Vision for Expanded Awareness as often as you can to become more energy sensitive, see or feel auras and heighten your psychic perception.

Visit
www.brightfuturenow.co.uk/meditations
to download or listen to a free audio mediation:
Meditation, Peripheral Vision

Meditate on the Light in the Head: an Adaptation of the Ancient Hindu and Huna Practices

Since energy flows where your attention goes, bringing your attention to the pineal gland will activate it. Meditation is focusing on one thing. Here we focus the mind on the light within. What we focus on, we expand. This meditation is designed to expand the light in you.

- Make the room as dark as possible.
- Close your eyes and bring your attention to your breathing.
- Deepen the in-breath and lengthen the out-breath.
- Relax the jaw.
- A longer out-breath tells the body it's time to relax.
- Bring your awareness to your space of the Third Eye.
- While you keep breathing, roll the eyes upward and to the right. Then roll the eyes upward and to the left. Then lift the eyes straight up as if to look at the sky. Focus on the light in the space between the centre of the eyebrows. Let the light come to you, welcome the light.

- If you can't see the light easily, then take your thumb and forefinger and press the eyeballs lightly from outside, upward, hold for five seconds. Let go – and watch the light.
- You may see spots of light or swirls of colour. Anything other than black is the light.
- Pay attention to the light. Now just let go, relax the eyes and watch the light.
- Draw down the light into the body with every breath.
- Expand the light into your aura/energy field.
- Focus on the light that expands your consciousness.
- Allow your awareness to expand into the periphery as you watch the light.
- Wider and wider into the nothingness, into the void.
- Enter into the void.
- Total oneness with the light.
- You are a being of light, of infinite potential.
- Feel your connection with the light.
- You are in the light. The light is in you.
- You are the light.
- Your true nature is love, joy, peace and creativity.
- Continue to meditate on the light.
- Slowly bring your awareness back, become more centred and grounded. Open your eyes and re-energise by taking a few deep breaths.

Visit
www.brightfuturenow.co.uk/meditations
to download or listen to a free audio meditation:
Meditate on the Light in the Head

Meditate in Stillness

This meditation has the purpose of connecting in quiet and stillness, of deep listening in openness to receive guidance. You can also take a question into your meditation. To the mind, the question is a reference beam that it shines into the hologram (or the akasha) to retrieve previously unknown data from the holographic memory bank (Judith, 2004).

Framework for your meditation

- Ground, connect with your guides and ask for protection, to be held in the light.
- Set your intention for the meditation.
- Breathe into the diaphragm; make the out-breath twice as long. Do this for a while to shift your nervous system. Effectively you shift beyond the three-dimensional ego-driven world.
- Connect with your Higher Self. Take a moment to feel the subtle energy shift.
- Meditate for a while in stillness.
- Ask your question.
- Listen quietly, sense deeply, remain open to receive guidance.
- Close down with gratitude.
- Ground.
- Capture any insights in your journal.
- Remain open to answers and guidance that may surface over the next few days.

Visit
www.brightfuturenow.co.uk/meditations
to download or listen to a free audio meditation:
Meditate in Stillness, Connecting with your Inner Guidance

Step 7: Master Your Higher Awareness

The seventh chakra is the first chakra outside the human body. Having practised expanded awareness and the gifts of the higher mind at Step 6, here we explore our connection with spirit.

Journey Through the Chakras: Crown Chakra

Colour	Purple
Location	Just above the head
Qualities and Functions of the Crown Chakra	The Crown Chakra is your connection to the higher spiritual realms. It has the qualities of unity, wisdom and higher consciousness. When activated and open, divine light flows through you, replenishing your entire being, empowering, informing and enlightening you. The full essence and power of your accumulated soul experiences are available here.
Key Functions for Mastery	• Mastering the Laws of Higher Awareness. • Mastering your integration into wholeness.

Master the Key Universal Laws of Higher Awareness

- *The Law of Reincarnation*: If there is anything unresolved or incomplete at the end of a lifetime, the soul can return in human form to resolve or complete it.

- *The Law of Ascension*: To ascend we must complete our karma, master the lessons of life, find balance, open our hearts to love and become one. When you lose the illusion of separation from your divine self, your vibration raises to the point of ascension. No longer does this mean that we leave the earth plane to live a refined ascended existence. We are meant to bring our loving energies to our everyday existence, becoming an example for others to emulate.
- *The Law of Oneness*: All is one and we are all one.

Healing and Wholeness

Here at the Crown Chakra, we have completed a journey. We have come full cycle. The journey is one of healing, growth, fulfilment, completion and preparation for ascension. You have come to heal the past, grown into your power, fulfilled the ego, moved beyond it, come to know love, your higher gifts and your higher purpose. Not only have you been healing this life, you have been healing unresolved issues from your past existences. That's the nature and opportunity of this life. We are tying all loose ends, finishing everything off and healing all of the past. Healing is achieving integration and wholeness – integrating your three minds into one. When the minds work in synergy as one integrated higher mind, it becomes still and expansive. Any thoughts are higher thoughts of pure inspiration and your mind is one with the universal mind, where infinite wisdom can be tapped.

Completion and Higher Awareness

When you heal all your past karma and master the lessons of illusions such as duality, fears, ego and projections, you can end the wheel of incarnation and choose to ascend. In the past we had to pass over to ascend. Now, for the first time in a grander scale are the energies right for us to ascend the ego and be our true higher selves here on Earth.

We can end the era of karma, move beyond learning through suffering and open up to a life of positive experience, creativity, love, joy and expansion. To do this, we have to heal all past negative emotions and overcome any perceived limiting beliefs. We have to bring all our unconscious wounds, programmes and projections into conscious awareness and continue to integrate more of our true higher selves. Anything that's still unresolved, your Crown Chakra energy can and will make known to you. Memories, emotions and limiting beliefs will continue to surface. When they do, they don't come up to haunt you. They come up to be healed and released. Recognise this as an opportunity for healing and integration. Use your meditations like *Ho'oponopono* and the Mindfulness Healing Meditation to bring anything that surfaces into reflection. Learn from it, then heal and release it. Also continue to release any fears and doubts, and come into the heart, embracing love and compassion. Bring your life into balance and set the intention that you are ready to ascend into wholeness.

The Mastermind-set

- I am whole and of one integrated higher mind.
- I am my true higher self.
- I am love, joy and peace.

Mastery Practices

- Continue to bring any unhealed memory, feeling or limiting belief that bubble up into conscious awareness, into reflection. Learn from it, forgive it, heal it, then release it. Follow the daily reflection practice and the Higher Self-Healing Meditation of Step 2.
- Meditate regularly to cultivate higher awareness.

Meditation

There was a time when the Crown Chakra was the completion of our evolutionary journey and the culmination of our wisdom. Now, so much more is opening up to us through the activation of the Sacred Chakras and the energetic opportunities and gifts that they offer. In Step 11 we will explore the details of connecting with your Higher Self. Here at the Crown, we just pause a while, reflect on our journey and bring ourselves into balance, wholeness and preparation for a whole new level of unfoldment.

Microcosmic Orbit: An Ancient Chi Kung and Yoga Energy Practice

- Ground and protect yourself by placing yourself in the light.
- Sit upright, contract the perineum, the pelvic floor muscles. Place the tip of your tongue on the roof of the mouth, behind the teeth.
- On inspiration, imagine a purple light coming down through your Crown Chakra and down the front of the body, through all the chakras to the Root Chakras at the base of the pelvis. Feel and see the purple light, revolving clockwise.
- Then raise the light, the energy by breathing it up the back of the spine to the top of the head, the Crown Chakra again. Follow the flow of the energy with your breath.
- Then with the out-breath, direct the light, the energy down the front through all the energy centres again towards the base.
- Continue the orbit again, repeating the circle several times.
- Enjoy the energy sensation of this balancing breathing practice.
- Over time, increase the practice to 36 orbits per meditation.
- You will feel energised, balanced, whole, uplifted and healthy.

- Complete the *Microcosmic Orbit Meditation* by grounding the energy.

Visit
www.brightfuturenow.co.uk/meditations
to download or listen to a free audio meditation:
Microcosmic Orbit Meditation

You can also use this *Chakra Balancing Meditation*, to anchor in your journey of growth so far and further prepare yourself for activating your higher Sacred Chakras.

Visit
www.brightfuturenow.co.uk/meditations
to download or listen to a free audio meditation:
Chakra Balancing Meditation

Take a moment to reflect on your own journey so far, on how it's prepared you with a healthy, balanced foundation upon which you can open up and integrate the higher energies of the Sacred Chakras into your being.

Step 8: Master the Laws of Energy

We are about to discover the essence of the Sacred Chakras. You have prepared yourself and laid the foundation with your advanced journey through the first seven chakras. Self-mastery becomes the foundation for spiritual mastery. The first step is to become conscious of who you are and then you can master the gifts and talents that you have. To be the Master of your own Self is to fully understand who you really are. It is a discovery of the wizard within, the inner guiding Light. In the next five Steps, as you open up to the sacred energies offered to you now, you will become a brilliant channel of light as you open up to your true magnificence. The energies that we are going to open up to are so powerful that we'll start with a strong sound foundation.

Journey Through the Chakras: Sacred Earth Star Chakra

Colour	White light of pure spirit
Location	Below your feet, in the ground
Qualities and Functions of the Sacred Earth Star Chakra	As a physical being on Earth, you have a unique connection with the ascending Earth. Your Earth Star Chakra is your personal link to the Earth's energy grid (described below) and the divine light contained within the Earth. When activated, your Earth Star Chakra expands in size and power, connecting you deep into the energy core of the Earth. The blueprint of your mission on Earth, will then be accessible and you'll be guided to where on the planet you are meant to be, to fulfil your unique role during this time when the Earth makes its evolutionary shift. The Earth Star Chakra is your advanced grounding and connection to the Earth. It's even more essential to stay grounded now that the high vibrational energies are coming in and we are becoming energetically more refined. Distinct from the Root Chakra, which is the grounding chakra of the seven-chakra system, the Earth Star Chakra is the grounding point for your entire extended chakra system. Through your Earth Star Chakra you feel deeply connected to your own energies, those of the Earth, your ancestral line and the universe. Through the Earth Star Chakra, you can connect to the higher consciousness grid around the Earth. Because this chakra contains the pure white light of spirit, as you connect to the inner energy grid of the Earth, you simultaneously link into the outer grid of the Earth; the new fifth-dimensional consciousness grid (elaborated below). Healing your Earth Star Chakra helps in healing the Earth. As we clear our Earth Star Chakra, we assist in clearing and balancing the energies of collective fear from the planet and we become part of the process of healing humanity.
Key Functions for Mastery	• Mastering the Universal Laws of Energy. • Mastering the grounding of the extended chakra system. • Connecting with nature and the sacred energy of the earth. • Anchoring in and living the new values; the new way of being on a new Earth.

Master the Key Universal Laws of Energy

- Everything is energy.
- Energy has quantity and quality. Quantity-wise, we can be overcharged or undercharged. Quality-wise, energy can be of a low dense vibration or of a high, refined vibration.
- We are energy manifested as form.
- Energy is always moving.

Everything is Energy

Like the Earth, we too have an electromagnetic field around us. Energetically, we are made the same as the Earth. In fact, galaxies, stars, planets, people, our DNA and cells are all based on the same energy design – spiralling, toroidal vortices are the primary energy pattern of the universe (Dannelley, 1995). Apart from your physical body, your energy field or aura consists of your subtle, energy bodies, namely your emotional body, your mental body and your spiritual body. Your four bodies are linked with the elements of fire, air, water and earth. This is our link with nature (see Figure 5 below). Everything is energy. Energy determines your sense of well-being, your quality of life, how you feel and how you connect and engage with others. Energy affects everything – your productivity, your creativity, your efficiency, your health and your sense of vitality and joy. Energy is the subtle essence of spirit before it manifests as form. Energy is the spark of spirit in you.

As above so below

While psychologists and philosophers have been searching for the seat of the soul and where and how it links to the body, the shamans of old knew that the energy field around the body is actually the soul. You are the light; you are spirit that has gradually lowered its vibrations until eventual manifestation in physical form.

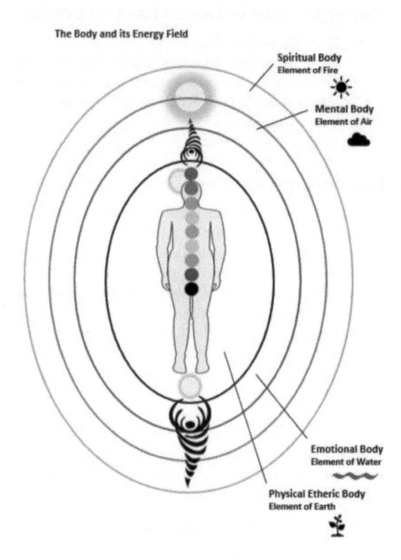

Figure 5: The Body and its Energy Field

The Earth's Consciousness Grid

The Earth's energy grid can be equated with our energy field and, just as we have meridian lines, so the Earth has energy lines called ley lines. In and around the inner core of the Earth is the inner energy grid which is connected via energy vortices to the outer grid around the Earth. Just as we change genetically and energetically in our evolution, so does the Earth. The Earth's energy grid has a unique geometric pattern. Evolution is also reflected in geometric patterns becoming more and more complex. Before the new consciousness grid came in place, the Earth's previous three-dimensional grid had a more simplistic limited geometric pattern. Consequently, we were energetically and consciously cut off from higher dimensions. It may well be that the legendary fall from the Garden of Eden was an energetic fall in consciousness. It may even be the same legend as the fall of Atlantis, a once highly advanced civilisation which came to its demise due to the abuse of higher power and higher gifts for self-gain and resulted in a fall in consciousness. Plato, who wrote about Atlantis, also came up with the basics of geometry, the Platonic Solids. It seems Plato had knowledge of the Earth's grid, as he spoke of 'the ideal body of the cosmos' being a synthesis of the Platonic Solids. Plato said 'The Earth itself looks from above, if you could see it, like those twelve-patched leather balls' (Dannelley, 1995). A dodecahedron is made up of 12 equal patches. When a dodecahedron is combined with the icosahedron, they form the synthesis of all Platonic Solids which we now refer to as the geometry of the new consciousness grid (Dannelley, 1995) – Plato's ideal body of the cosmos! The consciousness shift we are experiencing on Earth is reflected in a shift from the old limited three-dimensional consciousness grid to an expanded fifth-dimensional grid. The new fifth-dimensional grid has only just become activated and accessible to us, effectively connecting us with the higher consciousness planes of the universe once again. This means a stronger connection with spirit and access to higher knowledge once again.

Advanced Grounding and Connection with the Earth

The high vibrational energy of nature has a therapeutic, restorative healing effect on us. We are integrally part of nature. The cycles of the seasons, the moon and the planets have profound effects on us. Nature is constantly flowing through us as we breathe, drink water, eat food and soak up sun. We can heal ourselves by balancing the elements in our own bodies. Consciousness is in everything and everything is connected like a big web – the web of life.

The Mayan prophesies on the New World Age and the shift in human consciousness, predicted our return to nature and its natural cycles as an essential catalyst to the shift (Benedict, 2008). They also said, for us to truly connect and live with nature and its cycles again, we'll have to return to a 13-month lunar calendar.

As we bring our awareness back to the wonder of the natural world, we soon realise our fundamental interconnectedness. Everything is one and we are part of something much greater than us. Bringing our awareness back to nature lies at the heart of our happiness, and the well-being of all life on Earth (Thompson, 2013).

In the book *Earthing: The Most Important Health Discovery Ever* (2010), Ober, Sinatra and Zucker describe the natural healing benefits of direct contact with the earth by walking barefoot. The Earth's surface is alive with electrical energy that is continuously replenished by the sun and by lightning activity. The sole of the foot has 1,300 nerve ends that are designed to keep us in touch with the Earth and draw vital energy for nourishment and good health. Modern life has separated us from the nourishing energy and sensory connection with the earth. The result of the simple practice of walking barefoot, has striking, even transformational effects on people's health and vitality. The authors quote numerous examples of inflammatory-related disorders, fatigue, insomnia and chronic pain relieved, and even vanished as a result. Nature has a built-in intelligence, and everything is interlinked and connected. Restoring our immune system naturally may be another reason to return to nature.

The Mastermind-set

- We are one with nature
- We are the 'seed' people of the new paradigm.

Mastery Practices

Advanced Grounding Technique

Focus your attention on the Earth Star Chakra below your feet in the Earth. Visualise it like a disc of white light. Visualise spinning the disc in a clockwise direction and expand it out about the width of the body. Visualise it going down into the Earth like a cone-shaped vortex, connecting into the inner energy grid of the Earth. As it connects into the inner grid, the energy simultaneously runs upward along the connecting energy vortices, all the way up to the outer grid around the Earth; the new higher consciousness grid that connects us instantly to the universe and the higher cosmic forces. So, whilst you are perfectly grounded and connected to the inner grid of the Earth, you are simultaneously connected into the outer higher consciousness grid. You are both here and infinite expanded everywhere. This is such a powerful grounding practice, that it's best that you have your protection and intention in place beforehand.

Scanning Your Energy Field, Clearing and Maintaining Your Aura

- Ground, connect with your healing guides and set the intention for protection by placing yourself in the light.
- In your inner vision, scan your aura; your energy field; up and down, front and back, to the sides. Scan for holes, tears

and weakened areas. Scan for any darker areas. Is the colour around the head clear and light or is it like a grey cloud created by thought forms?

- Scan the rest of your energy field for darker spots or stains caused by feelings, stress, interactions, experiences, attachments or energy contamination.
- Do the scanning effortlessly. Let the picture form all by itself, let the shades and intuition just come to you. You can also ask your guides to show you what you need to be aware of.
- Ask your healing guides to remove any stains, any thought forms, dense energies or attachments by sending it into the light.
- Ask that any energy cords be dissolved.
- Witness the process of clearing.
- Sense the release.
- Now ask the guides to start an energy flush, sense it.
- Ask your guides to start an energy balance; that the chakra system be realigned – this can take ten minutes.
- Stay attuned, sensing, witnessing.
- Now ask the guides to close any auric holes or tears that may have resulted in the removal process and to strengthen any weak areas in the aura.
- Witness and affirm it is done and close down.
- Ground yourself.

Building the Light Bodies

Your light bodies; your aura is the energy imprint that creates the physical body. Energising and clearing the light bodies is an essential proactive investment in the physical health of the body. The light body is also the vehicle of your multi-dimensional self. To become more of your fifth-dimensional aspect, work to energise and build the light bodies. The microcosmic orbit breathing is one way of doing it. Another way is through energy work such as tai chi or yoga. Here is a simple yet very powerful meditative visualisation that I've learnt in tai chi. It has the effect of purifying, energising and expanding the light bodies:

- See yourself in a white light, breathing in the light until you become whiter and brighter. Bring your awareness to the lower *tan tien* in the area of the navel. Breathe into it whilst visualising a white blue light, the colour of the physical etheric body. Blue is also the colour of natural energy given off by trees and plants and vitalises the physical body. See the vital energy expanding from your *tan tien*, into your energy field like a light blue mist. See this blue light dissolving any discomforts in the body, offering you good health.

- Now bring your awareness to the Sacred Heart Centre. Breathe into the Sacred Heart and visualise a white pink light, the colour of the emotional body. As you breathe and energise this centre and the emotional body, see this pink radiance expand all around you. See it dissolve any stains in the emotional body as it expands out, lifting you up in positivity, love and joy.

- Finally bring your awareness to the mental body. See a golden sun in the centre of your head. Breathe and expand this golden light so it begins to radiate out from your head and fill your mental body. As it does so, it burns away any thoughts, and the mind becomes clear and still.

- See yourself now filled with this blue, pink and golden light radiating out from you into your energy bodies, uplifting and expanding your energy field and bringing you good health.

- Ground and bring your meditation to a close.

Anchoring in and Living the New Values: The New Way of Being on a New Earth

This shift from one era into another, brings a radical change in consciousness, a shift in our understanding. We begin to see things differently. As the new age unfolds, we are making a shift to a whole new values level. By practising these new values, you are being the change.

Table 2: New Era Values

Outgoing Values Age of Pisces (past 2,000 years)	New Age Values Age of Aquarius (coming 2,000 years)
Materialism	Spirituality; abundance; let go of ego
Competitive	Collaboration, sharing; cooperation; generosity; support
Success	Nurturing; goodwill
Exploitation	Sustainability; respect for natural resources, respect for Earth and everyone and everything
Scarcity	Self-sufficiency; return to simple living; minimalism; abundance
Separateness	Interconnectedness; oneness
Individualism	Community
Differences and imbalances: • Nations • Cultures • Borders • Religions • Gender	Commonality; equality; respect for all: • Common good • Global community • Fairness; integrity • Balanced male and female energy
Secrecy	Openness; honesty; transparency (live as if people can read your thoughts)
War; conflict	Peace; joy; harmony; compassion
Technology; science	Creativity; flexibility
Fear-based	Unconditional love
Dominance; autocracy	Empowerment of all
Fast pace	Slowed pace of life; youth; health

Fifth-Dimensional Living on a New Earth

We've just come out of a two-thousand-year-old astrological age of Pisces. It was a fear-based, patriarchal era of competitiveness, an era of conflict and war, driven by separation and differences – cultural, religious, political and gender differences. It was characterised by autocracy, dominance and secrecy. Greed resulted in exploitation of people, nations and natural resources. Motivated by individual success and materialism, our ever fast-paced lives became stressful and out of balance until a tipping point was reached. Something had to change.

We are just entering the new Aquarian age which is bringing in the much needed and long-awaited feminine qualities of support, sharing, nurturing, cooperation, generosity, equality, fairness and goodwill. The focus is shifting back to community, respect for all, the common good of all and respect for the Earth and its natural resources. There is a return to simple living, minimalism, self-sufficiency and sustainability. Exploitation, unfair systems and secrecy are now being challenged, fostering a spirit of openness, honesty and transparency. Disillusioned by the stressful chase after material gain, people are now slowing down, restoring balance, investing in their health and quality of life instead. The new era sees a return to peace, joy, harmony and compassion. On a global scale we may still see the chaotic outplay of the old era. As we adopt these more love-based qualities in ourselves, we create the tipping point into a new peaceful, loving, communal existence on Earth. We are here to usher in these feminine qualities. It is not about replacing the old yang, masculine way with a new yin, feminine way. It is about restoring the balance. We are already seeing a return to nature as many people enjoy planting their own food and enjoy sharing it abundantly.

The new values will see people living more and more in close connection with the environment, as self-sustained, cooperative communities. Perhaps we will invent healthier built technology, new means of travel, alternative energy sources, and a form of exchange, monetary, barter or otherwise, much healthier and viable than our current crumbling monetary system. The newly transformed Earth may well be a place of joy, peace, harmony and compassion beyond imagination. A place of generosity, trust, openness and positive support for everyone.

As fifth-dimensional beings we will be energetically transformed, have higher psychic attainments, be motivated to serve, support and care for all, joyfully. Living in unity, we will do only what is for the highest good of everyone and the planet. We will care for the Earth and be as one, interconnected whole, responding to the needs of others. Free from ego and judgement. Free from any power struggle and personal agenda. Rather than working purely for financial survival out of fear and insecurity, we will do the work that satisfies our soul. People will be motivated by love, creative expression, the desire to help and serve. The old lack mindset gone, we will experience true abundance. Thought will manifest instantly, and we will have everything we need. Happy to share everything, we may not necessarily have to possess and own things like cars. Our hearts will be open. We will enjoy recovered youth and health as our natural state.

Perhaps as the ancients predicted, we will move beyond our dependence on clock-time and technology. As we open up to the higher abilities of the higher mind, we will use our minds to do the things we use our gadgets to do for us now. We will sense others' needs intuitively and communicate telepathically. To do this, our minds will need to be unguarded, open and transparent. How pure will we have to be to have transparent minds, happy for others to pick up on our every thought? This is a mere glimpse of the new heaven on earth we are here to establish.

Meditation

Visualising and Anchoring in the New Earth

- If you can do this meditation outside at least to start with, you will be able to really connect with the Earth's nourishing energy. This practice will have a powerful activation effect on your Earth Star Chakra, something you can bring about with focused intention.

- Connect with your guides and ask for protection, to be held in the highest light.
- Ground through the Earth Star Chakra as described above.
- See yourself as a perfect conduit of light, channelling the high vibrational heavenly light into the Earth. Just by being here you are bringing in the light. That's your purpose.
- Visualise the New Earth, the kind of place you want to live in and pass on to the generations to come. By envisioning it, you create it together with many lightworkers around the world, all holding a higher vision. Feel the love, joy, sense of community and oneness. Anchor in your vision with the light you are channelling into the Earth.
- Close down your meditation with the intention to stay grounded and connected.

Visit
www.brightfuturenow.co.uk/meditations
to download or listen to a free audio meditation:
Visualising and Anchoring in the New Earth

Step 9: Master the Laws of Karma

In Step 9 we face another opportunity for healing – healing at an advanced level. Here we also uncover the essential purpose of this current life on Earth during this time of a consciousness shift. To usher in this shift, many lightworkers have come in, born into specific families and clothed themselves with those family patterns. As you heal these patterns in yourself, you heal family karma. This is a key role of lightworkers. In the process you assist in uplifting the planet. Regression hypnotherapist, Dolores Cannon, described the call that the lightworkers responded to when they came to this planet to assist in a mass awakening of humanity, and to prepare humanity for the arrival of the fifth-dimensional Earth. She found remarkable common themes of the many people she regressed under hypnosis and in her book, *Three Waves of Volunteers and the New Earth* (2011), she describes how these volunteers came to the planet in three waves of souls since the mid-1950s. These three waves of souls are often called the Indigo, Crystal and Rainbow children. We usher in change through inner work more than outward action.

Journey Through the Chakras: Sacred Navel Chakra

Colour	Light blue
Location	At the navel, between the Sacral Chakra and the Solar Plexus
Qualities and Functions of the Sacred Navel Chakra	The Navel Chakra is your storehouse of energy. In Chi Kung it is named the Tan Tien, the location of the original chi, the life force energy in the body. This is your true inner energy core. In the same way as the Navel Chakra stores vital energy, it is also the storehouse for the dense karmic programmes you brought in, or were born into, to take on and bring healing to the ancestral line, even whole communities. This is a key chakra for advanced healing. Once cleared, a major shift in healing is achieved and a lightness of energy sets in. The Navel Chakra holds the energy for physical health, vitality and manifestation.
Key Functions for Mastery	• Mastering the Laws of Karma and Non-judgement. • Healing karmic patterns. • Ancestral healing. • Moving beyond the wheel of karma.

Master the Key Universal Laws of Karma

- *The Law of Karma; the Law of Cause and Effect*: As you give, so you receive.
- *The Law of Non-Judgement*: Judgement is a human invention of duality.
- *The Law of Reincarnation*: If there is anything unresolved or incomplete at the end of a lifetime, the soul can return in human form to resolve or complete it.
- *The Law of Ascension*: To ascend we must complete our karma, master the lessons of life, find balance, open our hearts to love and become one. When you lose the illusion of separation from your divine self, your vibration raises to the point of ascension. No longer does this mean that we leave the earth plane to live a refined ascended existence. We are meant to bring our loving energies to our everyday existence, becoming an example for others to emulate.

Significance of This Time

We chose to reincarnate during this time on Earth because we wanted to finish up our own unresolved business. In doing so, we also heal the ancestral line. We are working towards ascension and ascension can indeed be achieved in this lifetime. Healing karma is a key focus of our healing journey today, and so is ancestral healing. I believe that's a key life purpose for many of us. As we clear up our karma and move beyond duality and fear, we uplift the whole. All consciousness is connected and ultimately everyone benefits. We can then evolve in consciousness into the true oneness of love, joy, peace, positivity and creativity.

About Karma

Karma is the direct expression of the Law of Cause and Effect. The scientific equivalent of this law teaches that 'for every action there is an equal and opposite reaction'. Like all Laws, it's beautifully built into the fabric of the universe to maintain balance objectively. There is no judgement, reward or punishment involved. Karma is about balanced experience. Our actions have consequences. Through experiences and consequences, we gain wisdom. Especially when we take full responsibility for everything playing out in our universe. The Law of Cause and Effect continues to nudge us towards change, raising our consciousness to ever greater heights. Our goal is to release any negativity and become masters of positive thoughts and actions. The Law of Cause and Effect works towards your evolution, as you evolve from unconscious to conscious, from ego to beyond ego and finally to fulfilling the highest potential of your true Higher Self. Ultimately, everything that happens, happens for your evolution.

Pre-Birth Planning

An awareness of pre-birth planning helps us to see our experiences and interactions from a perspective of deeper purpose, learning and growth.

Your family is your karma. Your soul chooses your family before you are born (Cooper, 2000). Your family is part of your soul group. Your soul group goes wider and involves other significant relationships in your life. A soul group is a collection of souls who are more or less at the same evolutionary stage, and who incarnate together repeatedly, playing every conceivable role for one another (Schwartz, 2012). We co-plan our life purpose and it includes many individual agreements to meet and work with certain people in certain places at certain times. So, you have made commitments, you have been assigned tasks, and agreed on lessons to learn to fulfil your divine potential. As you resolve your own karmic patterns, you often heal family karma. In the process you also assist in lifting planetary vibrations.

We are often born into the exact opposite of what we want to become. You may be born into a family that values intellect over emotions for you to ultimately grow in compassion. You may experience criticism and judgement as you grow up, so that you can learn to liberate yourself from opinions and grow in the confidence to follow your own path. You may be born into poverty to embrace abundance. You may be born into the perpetuation of victimhood to find your own empowerment. You may be born in conflict to help liberate whole communities and find peace.

Michael Talbot (1991) offers a great perspective on life's design and purpose in his book *The Holographic Universe*. Comprehensive research found that hypnotised individuals and young children often display memory of reincarnation. Out of numerous interviews and experiments, remarkable similarities emerged:

- Numerous previous lives are recalled – as many as 25.
- Gender is not specific to the soul, one could have previous lives of the opposite sex.
- The purpose of life is to evolve and learn, a process facilitated through multiple existences.
- There is an interim between lives that is a dazzling light-filled realm from where they plan their next life with a sense

of moral obligation, to literally sketch out the important events and circumstances that would befall them in future.

- They would choose to be reborn with people whom they feel they had wronged in a previous life to make amends for their actions.
- They planned pleasant encounters with soul mates – individuals with whom they build loving and mutually beneficial relationships over many lifetimes.
- They scheduled 'accidental' events to fulfil lessons and purposes – not always pleasant but that would help with a deeper understanding of the meaning of life.
- Our unconscious mind is not only aware of the rough outline of our destiny but actually steers us towards its fulfilment.
- We choose our earthly circumstances – nothing is random or inappropriate.
- The future is only roughly outlined and still subject to change.
- We are frequently reborn with individuals we have known in previous existences. The guiding force behind our choices is often affection or a sense of indebtedness.
- Personal responsibility is therefore the arbiter of our fate; not chance.

Ancestral Healing

We used to think that our genes control us; that certain conditions run in the family and that we are destined to have the same conditions and illnesses passed on to us. This belief practically makes us a victim of our genes. Thanks to cellular biologist Bruce Lipton's work, *The Biology of Beliefs* (2005), we now know that DNA is simply on and off switches. These DNA switches respond to signals in the environment, rather than our genetic inheritance. Furthermore, the DNA responds to our thoughts and our perceptions of the environment. Our consciousness – whether we feel safe or threatened – turns the stress response on or off. Every thought impacts on your cells. Your genetic biology is really run by your consciousness; your thoughts and perceptions.

So, genetic conditions aren't passed on to us. What is passed on to us is the memory. Genetic memory can go back three or four generations. In the cells and in the energy field that binds us together are thought forms, belief systems, patterns, habits, emotions and information that have been stored by past generations for centuries. Therefore, many things that we feel and do are governed not just by our own beliefs but by what our ancestors experienced and believed as well. Some of these beliefs are useful and some not. We have to question our beliefs, their relevance and usefulness all the time.

Cynthia was a client I worked with for a while. One of the issues she discussed was a repeated cycle of not being able to afford basic things. In exploring this, we found an ancestral link that is actually quite common to many of us. Cynthia was very sparing, mindful not to waste anything. Although a good practice, there was an underlying scarcity mindset underpinning her behaviour. During Cynthia's healing journey, we discovered that the root cause goes back to her grandmother who wouldn't waste a crumb, a value that she imprinted on her children and grandchildren. Her grandmother lived through the Great Depression and the Second World War when food was severely rationed. This was the root cause of Cynthia's scarcity mindset even today. Clearing the old energies and beliefs, Cynthia was free to adopt and live by her own new empowering beliefs, allowing her to be receptive to an inflow of abundance in her own life.

When you heal, release and change such limiting beliefs, you change the DNA through the on/off switches, not just for yourself, but also your siblings, parents, children and extended family. Memory is also stored in the unconscious mind, such as the core beliefs we grew up with. Past life memory can also be stored in the etheric energy field (Edwards, 2010). When you heal for example your anger, it releases from the energy field that you share with generations of your ancestral line. So, it releases for them too and brings profound healing even if they have already passed over. You also heal your children and grandchildren that way.

Diane came for therapy after she'd been diagnosed with cancer. She didn't ask me to assist her in healing the cancer. She just said: 'I want to heal the anger that has been passed on from one generation to another in my family. I want to stop the cycle here and free my children and grandchildren from it'. That's profound insight on her behalf, and a clear awareness of her role and responsibility in healing the family. Serving this purpose was of key importance for her.

Many lightworkers are here to usher in the change through inner work and adopting the new era values as described in Step 8. Part of our purpose at this time is to transmute all negative energy and challenge societal taboos and beliefs about what's right and wrong. You are an energy converter. As you let go of your own fear-based limiting beliefs, you uplift and liberate others. Your purpose may be to heal blocked emotions, to transmute all unresolved negative energies from past lives and to integrate it into the whole of your being. The work of soul retrieval is a key aspect of this integration.

Soul Retrieval

Traumas and significant emotional experiences of the past can create soul loss. Some of your energy or an aspect of you got left behind in the event. Soul loss can be as a result of attachments to people or places, energy leakages or lost energy often as a result of trauma, even surgery. Examples of lost aspects are your sense of fun, light-heartedness, sense of humour, free-spiritedness, sense of caring (feeling you can't be bothered), loss of childlike innocence or loss of joy. Soul loss can happen when you feel great loss with someone's passing. Lost parts can appear to you in dreams about past experiences too. Take note of these messages and attend to any unfinished business of your healing process.

When these soul fragments are retrieved and integrated, you can feel energised, light and whole again. The effects can be dramatic. You may feel a shift in your world view, beliefs or attitudes. You may experience drastic life changes as a result, such as a job change, a house move, or a change in relationships. Wholeness is healing. If you feel some aspect of you is lost or stuck in the past, the meditation at the end of this Step will facilitate this powerful process of soul retrieval for you.

In his book *Soul Retrieval* (2005), Alberto Villoldo, describes original and ancestral wounds. Ancestral wounds can also be passed down from one generation to the next, perhaps endured during the Holocaust, a revolution or war time as described above. Original wounds are described as the loss of innocence that every child experiences as they grow up. Original wounds can be more the result of our perception at the time, rather than the actual event.

A typical experience was the work with my client, Janet. Janet discovered that her deep-seated feeling of shame went back to being told off by a teacher in front of the class for something very minor. In her healing journey, she could see her young self standing in front of the class. She could feel the feelings of shame very strongly. We went through the reflection and learning process to bring new perspectives and insights to this event, release the shame and retrieve her self-esteem. When it was time to return, Janet felt a strong urge to bring her child-self of this event back with her. We visualised bringing her in, the two (Janet of today and her child-self) merging into one again. She felt a vital energy and her natural confidence returning. Janet felt a weight lifting off her chest as the old emotions released. Janet retrieved her lost soul aspect and felt whole again.

How Do You Know Your Karma?

Karma often runs in a family like patterns of behaviour. If you want to know what your karma is, identify the challenges you are experiencing. They could be challenging relationships, repeating cycles of experiences, addictions, undesirable habits, negative emotions and limiting beliefs. Common karmic patterns are fear of rejection, fear of failure, fear of success, low self-esteem, self-doubt, lack of confidence, disorganisation, commitment phobia, being out of balance (head and heart; family and business; self and others), not trusting others, not trusting your inner knowing; your intuition; and not believing you deserve abundance. Karma may also be the things you avoid like speaking up for yourself, standing your ground, asserting yourself and your boundaries. We often have to work through our challenges to step into our gifts. Your karma is your greatest gift. Like a two-sided coin, karma is the flip side of your gift. Your gifts are where your fears lie. If for example you feel called to teach and you avoid it because you fear public speaking, that's your karma that needs resolving. Avoidance creates repeated cycles such as financial debt or abusive relationships. The sooner you face your fears and resolve your karma, the sooner you can step into your true gift, your power, your greatness and your joy.

Mastery is knowing your life lessons, overcoming them and stepping through them into your true higher gifts

We are at a turning point in history and this is a crucial lifetime for re-balancing. A lot is being crammed in as we are clearing thousands of years of outdated conditioning. Processing our individual and collective karma is our essential work right now. Chris Thomas, in *The Journey Home* (1998) describes how this ending of the process of karma means that we are finally able to begin the process of consciousness integration; of integrating the Higher Self fully into the physical body.

The time of learning through suffering is over. The wheel of karma is coming to an end. It has served its purpose. Karma is the result of the duality that we experience in the three-dimensional world where we learn through opposites. The new fifth-dimensional experience is one of unity. As we move into unity consciousness, we move beyond duality and learning through karma. Then we are free to open up to the magic of life and learn through curiosity, creativity, love and positive experiences.

We still have to watch the ego. The ego is attached to suffering. It has been running a programme of suffering for so long, it doesn't know another way. We have to watch this ingrained programme and as we integrate the ego into wholeness, reassure it that there is another way; a way of joy and love. We may have to remind ourselves of this often until learning through positive, joyful experiences becomes our effortless new habit.

Children born today have greater awareness and knowledge. These children are highly advanced and are now starting to come in free from karma. They are highly refined and sensitive. They can still be impacted by our karma, emotions and societal beliefs. We have the responsibility to support these angels on Earth. They come to do great work. They are the future of mankind, the future of the new homo luminous.

The Mastermind-set

- By healing myself, I heal the ancestral line and the planet.
- When I resolve my karma, I can finally bring karma to an end.
- The end of karma is the start of love, peace, abundance and positive growth experience.
- As I identify and end the suffering programme, I open up to living joyfully and magically.

Mastery Practices

Energy Visualisations

Metaphysically, you can generate energy by visualising the original source energy in your Navel Chakra like a ball of light-blue light. Breathe into the Navel Chakra, energising it. Visualise expanding the ball of blue light to fill the whole of the physical body, even beyond into your energy field. This practice replenishes your storehouse of energy and revitalises you.

When you walk in nature, make sweeping movements with your hands towards your Navel Chakra to revitalise yourself with the pure energy of nature. Visualise gathering in and storing pure light-blue energy in your Navel Chakra. Do this with respect and gratitude to the trees and plant life. Feel yourself nourished and energised.

Meditation

Ancestral Healing and Soul Retrieval with *Ho'oponopono*

- Ground through your Earth Star Chakra as described in Step 8. Connect with your healing guides. Set the intention for your meditation and ask for assistance with this powerful healing.
- Visualise the timelines of all your existences like the web of life. Perhaps you even see it multi-dimensionally like a 'spirally web'. See yourself standing in the centre of the web of life.
- Connect with source, with divine light. See yourself in a source of light; an infinite source of love and healing. You may visualise this light with a golden pink hue. Take this healing light into all of your being. Draw down this bright divine healing light into your cells and into your energy field. This is the light that heals, informs, transforms, enlightens,

energises and uplifts you – the light to heal and purify all chakras, endocrine glands, nervous system, organs, tissue, cells and DNA. See yourself becoming lighter and brighter. Feel the warmth and love of this healing light. Fill yourself up to overflowing. Then, channel this infinite source of love and healing light from your heart to flow down the web. Witness the entire web of life lighting up.

- Now, create a platform in your mind and invite family and members of your soul family to come and meet with you here. Together you've pre-planned your experiences, your challenges. Thank them for acting out their roles. It must have been challenging for them too. Thank them for the lessons and opportunities of growth. You can have a discussion with them in your mind, individually or as a group, clearing any issues.

- Say: I'm sorry, please forgive me. I love you. I thank you. Repeat the mantra *Ho'oponopono* until the negative feelings dissolve. When the forgiveness is done, the energetic cords will dissolve, and they will float off the platform, becoming one with the light.

- Call up ancestors of past generations, back seven to ten generations, some of whom you may know, others you may not, just let your Unconscious and Higher Conscious Minds who know the connections call them up. You can have a discussion with them in your mind, individually or as a group, clearing any issues.

- Say to them: I'm sorry, please forgive me. I love you. I thank you. Repeat the mantra *Ho'oponopono* until the feelings dissolve. When the forgiveness is done, the energetic cords will dissolve, and they will float off the platform, becoming one with the light.

- Call up yourself from significant other lifetimes. You may have an awareness or feeling about some of such experiences, of others you may not, just let your Unconscious and

Higher Conscious Minds, who know of the experiences and energies, call them up. You can have a discussion with these versions of yourself in your mind. Examples may be the young headstrong child you once were or the rebellious teenager, or the angry you or the shy you or the sad self who may have experienced losses. Vague memories, feelings or images may surface or not.

- Say to yourself: I'm sorry, please forgive me. I love you. I thank you. Repeat the mantra *Ho'oponopono* until the feelings dissolve. When the forgiveness is done, you may want to bring these aspects of yourself back into full integration. See yourself embracing, for example, the rebellious teenager, taking her inside of you, bringing your soul fragments back, feeling your energy coming back to you as you become one and whole again.

- As we clear ourselves to deeper and deeper levels, it allows us to take on more of the higher vibrational light, and more of your DNA activates, allowing greater access to memory of who you truly are and what you are capable of.

- Feel yourself becoming integrated, healed, back into wholeness. Intend and ask that your Sacred Navel Chakra become activated and light-filled.

- As you become more light-filled, more of your Higher Self can enter and reside in the physical body, activating the higher abilities of your higher mind: telepathic communication, psychic abilities, intuition, inner knowing, distant healing, clear-seeing, clear-hearing, clear-knowing, remembering the wisdom of the ancients, our ancestors who have been waiting eagerly for our awakening.

- Being whole and integrated, you can now connect into the web of life, the interconnectedness of everything, in a whole new powerful way – ready to use your true power and higher abilities to usher in the new earth. Catch a glimpse, set your intention for the new earth, a place where we can all dwell as our true Higher Selves.

- As you bring yourself back, do so as your whole integrated Higher Self, set the intention to live as your Higher Self, from the heart, and in this way, you are being the change, living the enlightened new earth right now.

Visit
www.brightfuturenow.co.uk/meditations
to download or listen to a free audio meditation:
Ancestral Healing and Soul Retrieval, with Ho'oponopono

Healing Childhood Emotions

Emotions are stored in us as a cluster or a gestalt. To heal past emotions, it's always good to find the root cause, learn from it (karma is learning) and then release the entire cluster. This meditation facilitates that process wonderfully and you can repeat it whenever you feel emotions rising.

Visit
www.brightfuturenow.co.uk/meditations
to download or listen to a free audio meditation:
Healing Childhood Emotions

Cutting from Tribal Connections

We were born into a tribe; a culture with a set of beliefs and values, some of which are useful and some not. The tribe has its own ideas of your roles and responsibilities and can place certain expectations on you. To evolve into true mastership, you want to be free from the tribal consciousness that can hold you back. This meditation will assist you to separate your consciousness from that of the tribe, so that you can stand in your own right, power and purpose.

Visit
www.brightfuturenow.co.uk/meditations
to download or listen to a free audio meditation:
Cutting from Tribal Connections

Step 10: Master Heart-Based Consciousness

The new consciousness is heart-based consciousness. We've been living in our heads for too long, valuing intellect over feelings. Now, as we make this evolutionary shift, we are coming home to the sacred heart, activating compassion and unconditional love.

Journey Through the Chakras: Sacred Higher Heart

Colour	Pink
Location	In the centre of your being, just above the Heart Chakra
Qualities and Functions of the Sacred Higher Heart Chakra	When activated you feel unconditional love and compassion for everyone and everything. Heart-based consciousness and group consciousness are the qualities of the Higher Heart. The heart-mind is by far more powerful than the brain as it receives information first and then passes it to the brain.
Key Functions for Mastery	• Mastering the Universal Laws of Divine Love and Oneness. • Mastering heart-based consciousness. • Mastering group consciousness. • Mastering heart expansion. • Living in the heart and making true decisions with your heart-mind from a basis of love and intuitive guidance, are key mastery practices of this chakra. The Sacred Higher Heart is the gateway to divine love and divine consciousness.

Master the Universal Laws of Divine Love and Oneness

- *The Law of Divine Love*: Love is divine power.
- *The Law of Unity*: We are all connected, all bearing the seed of divinity. This is the way we started, and the way we develop into eternity. When we experience great soul growth, in some small but profound manner, all benefit. All substance in this Universe flows to us and through us. We are One.

Mastering Heart-Based Consciousness

Heart coherence is a state achieved when you shift your focus into the heart and activate heart-based feelings such as love, caring and appreciation. According to research done by the HeartMath Institute, heart coherence reduces stress and restores health. 'Coherence is the state when the heart, mind and emotions are in energetic alignment and cooperation', HeartMath Institute Research Director Dr Rollin McCraty says. 'It is a state that builds resilience – personal energy is accumulated, not wasted – leaving more energy to manifest intentions and harmonious outcomes' (www.heartmath. org and www.heartmath.co.uk).

In western society we have valued the brain and its logical intellect over emotions for far too long. We seem to have overlooked the power of the heart. According to this latest research, the heart-brain is more powerful than the head-brain and has a vastly expanded electromagnetic field; much bigger than the head-brain and it extends several feet from the body. Our heart energy therefore dramatically affects those around us. When in this space you are more expansive, resourceful, connected and in a state of flow. The heart-brain seems instinctive and intuitive as it senses information in the environment before the cranial brain – and even before it happens. This is your own system of future precognition. It makes sense therefore to make decisions from the heart, intuitively; honouring that gut-feel. Heart-based consciousness is the new fifth-dimensional way of being.

At the Institute of HeartMath, experimentation with positive intent has shown a boost in the immune system. Negative thoughts like anger, depression, blame and frustration, have been found to suppress the immune system. Participants in a state of heart coherence were able to unwind DNA being observed under a microscope further away. They experimented further with a group of 28 researchers each holding a vial of DNA, while focusing on positive or negative emotions. When they focused on positive emotions such as love, joy, gratitude and appreciation, the DNA strands started relaxing and unwinding. When they generated negative fear-related thoughts the DNA tightened up and became shorter, some of the genes were shut down, limiting the range of possibilities we can tap and choose from.

Dr Masaru Emoto's intention experiment proved the same. Dr Emoto, author of *The Hidden Messages in Water* (2004), said that human consciousness has an effect on the molecular structure of water. He performed a series of experiments observing the physical effect of words, prayers, music and environment on water. The water would then be frozen to form crystalline structures. The crystalline structure of the water imprinted with positive words was far more symmetrical and aesthetically pleasing than those imprinted with dark, negative phrases. If our words and thoughts have this effect on water crystals, just imagine what kind of effect they have on people, considering we are 70 per cent water.

By being more love and light-filled, you affect the world profoundly. The master doesn't change the world by battling with external events. Instead, true mastery is healing and forgiving your inner perceptions of the world and changing judgemental and fear-related perceptions to loving ones, remaining non-attached and compassionate. The master works on the source of the problem, the mind. Mastery is restoring your mind to its natural condition of love and light.

Fifth-Dimensional Consciousness

The Higher Heart is all about fifth-dimensional consciousness – transformation of fear to love, shifting from head to heart, from separation and ego to true unity. The three-dimensional Earth, the plane of karma, is where we experience the dualities of light and dark, good and bad, right and wrong, other and self – all the opposites. We learn and gain great insights through experiencing duality. To move into fifth-dimensional unity consciousness, we have to integrate all duality in us: head and heart, ego and true self, fear and love. We also have to evolve our consciousness beyond any idea of good and bad or right and wrong or you and me or past and future. The fifth dimension is one of integrated unity, pure source light and unconditional love. Here we live beyond linear time, in the joy and expansion of the moment of now. To enter this plane fully, we have to be free from fear and any limiting beliefs. This is the plane of our Higher Self and of infinite potential. Living as a fully integrated fifth-dimensional being means the Higher Self is fully integrated into your being. Until you are fully integrated, the Higher Self will come in and out of your being. When you are fully fifth dimensional, you are in the flow of life, trust your journey and embrace the synchronicities of life, knowing you are perfectly guided on your path. In the fifth dimension, thoughts manifest effortlessly and instantly. It is the plane of abundance and infinite possibilities. Here you live from your heart and all your actions are motivated by unconditional love. It is the plane of unity consciousness, of oneness where we feel the connection with pure source energy and with everyone and everything. These are the qualities of the Sacred Higher Heart.

What about the fourth dimension, you may ask? The fourth dimension is the plane of the Unconscious Mind where we begin to work with our feelings and intuition. It's not a destination, it's simply a passage way through to the fifth dimension of our Higher Self. These planes of existence aren't places, they are levels of consciousness.

The Sacred Higher Heart is a gateway to higher consciousness. Through love, acceptance, forgiveness, gratitude, compassion and joy, you open the heart and naturally expand your energy field, your field of consciousness, and feel your connection with everyone and everything. In a state of heart coherence your good health and youthfulness naturally returns.

The Healing and Creative Power of Love

Creating and healing the fifth-dimensional way is very quick and powerful. Because the fifth dimension is perfection, creating and healing this way is not about correcting or fixing things. Instead, you create a whole new reality of perfection that make the previous condition obsolete.

***

Jane shared an inspiring example of the creative healing power of the Sacred Heart. Jane's daughter Kate who visited from Chester travelled back home by train. An incident on the train lines cause delays and rerouted her journey several times. She ended up in Manchester late evening after what seemed like an endless journey. Jane received a text from Kate saying, 'I've been on five trains and am currently waiting at Manchester, hoping for a train, but there doesn't seem to be any more trains to Chester'. Kate watched a number of trains passing through without stopping. Jane went within to send Kate healing light. She first asked Kate's Higher Self for permission. Then she visualised Kate encircled in golden light and asked her angels and healing guides to step in and help her. She visualised Kate stepping onto a train back to Chester, in a taxi, then home and in bed. She thanked the guides and closed down. Then she sent Kate a text message, 'I've just sent you positive light, your train is on its way now'. Just as Kate received this message from her mum, the overhead station announcement came on and said, 'The next train does not stop here please stand back'. The train came in and then, unexpectedly stopped and changed its destination to Chester! Seconds later Kate informed her mum that she was on the train, on her way home. Kate said, 'The train came in literally the same second I received your message!' Jane achieved this instant magical result through the power of love and the fifth-dimensional high vibration of magic and miracles. True mastery, and something anyone can do when acting with power, love and positive belief.

***

Mastery is embracing the power of love

The Mastermind-set

- In the heart, I am at one, connected to all.
- Every challenge is an opportunity for healing.
- I welcome joy into my life.
- I learn, grow and evolve through love, positivity and creativity.

Mastery Practices

Heart Expansion
In your meditation, bring your awareness in to the Sacred Heart centre. Breathe into it and expand the electromagnetic field of your heart centre. Feel yourself connecting to source.

Group Activity
Embrace the power of group activity such as group meditation, group healing and community projects. Intend that your every activity is for the highest and greatest good of all.

Healing

Bring healing to yourself, others and the planet through visualising, intention and blessing. You can channel healing light through your hands, from your heart and through your eyes. Healing takes place when loving high-frequency light transmutes negativity and disease. Healing can be sent over vast distances. Respecting free will, ask permission from their Higher Self. Visualise the person in a bright white or golden healing light and imagine the light filling their aura. Intend that the healing light is in their highest and greatest good. Affirm that you see them whole and in a perfect state of health. With gratitude, close down and separate yourself from the person energetically again. Detach from the outcome, accepting what will be, will be for their greatest good.

***

Upliftment

Practice the Inner Smile. This simple practice comes from the Taoist teachings. When we smile it is because we feel joy and happiness. Smiling connects us to a sense of life as light and fun. It is spontaneous and gives us a feeling of being uplifted. Smiling helps your body release good hormones. It's a gift.

Sit comfortably. Close your eyes. Take a moment to breathe and relax your body letting go of tension in the muscles. Let the word 'smile' float to the surface of your mind. You may find it easier to think of someone you care about and in your mind smile at them. It may be a person, a child, an animal or even a beautiful sunset or a walk in nature. Focus your mind on the feeling associated with the smile. Be aware of the positive, uplifting nature of this in your body. If you feel it in a particular part of the body let the mind rest in this area and then, breathing gently, let the feeling expand to fill the whole of you. Top to toe. Let that lightness of the inner smile fill your being, and rest in the joy of it.

Smile for yourself, smile for others, smile for life. Love your Inner Smile.

Contributed by Sue Keady, Tai Chi Teacher

***

Meditation

Shifting into the Heart

- Ground, connect and protect yourself by placing yourself in the light through intent.
- Relax, become aware of your breathing. Begin to deepen the in-breath and make the out-breath twice as long.
- Take note of what is going on in the mind, just noticing. Begin to still the mind using the breath – breathe out all the business, let it go. Let the world and its issues fade away as you go inside.
- Become aware of your body. Spend a moment in gratitude for the body and all its automatic processes – for the Unconscious Mind, keeping you energised and healthy, naturally. Give thanks to the body. Relax the body.
- Become aware of your feelings, your emotions. How are you feeling today? Not judging in any way, just taking note.
- Now, shift beyond these feelings.
- Shift your awareness into the heart. Place the palm of your one hand on your heart. Take your consciousness/attention in to the heart. Surrender the ego to the heart. Breathe into the heart. Hear and feel your heartbeat. Begin to relax the heart area, feel it becoming warm as you open the heart. Spread that warmth throughout the body.
- Your heart is the centre of your intuition, where your inspiration and ideas come from when you are relaxed; your

imagination opens up and you can be infinitely creative. Your heart is the centre of love and peace. Your Sacred Higher Heart raises these qualities to those of unconditional love, compassion and pure joy.

- Spend a few moments in love, appreciation and gratitude for who you are. You are totally unique and immensely valuable. Your life has a special meaning and purpose, one that only you can fulfil.

- Feel your heart at peace and know your mind is in the service of your heart. All is well.

- Allow your awareness to expand beyond yourself. The electromagnetic field of your heart will do so naturally.

- Expand your awareness wider and wider, to fill the room where you are. Expand your awareness beyond the room, beyond the towns and cities, beyond mother earth, beyond the solar system, into the wide universe, taking in everything. Notice that everything is just one thing, of which you are one.

- Enter a state of oneness with everyone and everything.

- Feel unconditional love for all living beings.

- Here at the heart you are connected to life itself, your source of energy and good health.

- Here you are safe and can trust safely who you are becoming.

- Your true nature is love, joy and peace.

- Your Sacred Higher Heart is a gateway to higher consciousness, where you have access to wisdom and your untapped potential.

- You have access to abundant inner resources. When you are yourself, you are more powerful than you can imagine.

- Notice how you have shifted into a relaxed state of being – feeling at peace, in the moment, free from the past, out of the future, free from fears and doubt, free to be your magnificent self.

- Through the practice of true forgiveness, unconditional love, joy, and heart expansion, you activate your Sacred Higher Heart.
- As you slowly begin to bring yourself back, do so with the intention of staying in this expanded, relaxed state – alive, energised and yet at ease and with creative energy flowing through you.
- Take a deep breath and a stretch.
- Ground yourself back in the body.

Visit
www.brightfuturenow.co.uk/meditations
to download or listen to a free audio meditation:
Shifting into the Heart

Step 11: Master Your Higher Consciousness

The journey of mastery is one of discovering and fulfilling your true Higher Self. As we evolve from our limiting three-dimensional consciousness and open up to our innate gifts of the higher mind, we can claim our inherent gifts, anchor in our higher consciousness and live as our true Higher Selves. The new higher vibrational light that has been coming in, enables you to embody more of your Higher Self and make this evolutionary shift of living as your True Higher Self on a New Earth.

Master the Universal Laws of Higher Consciousness

- *The Law of Meditation*: This Law encourages us to connect with our higher, inner selves, and connects the mind, body, soul and spirit. Meditation allows our divine selves to expand and grow. Meditation brings about balance and promotes the holistic healing of mind, body and soul.
- *The Law of Oneness*: All is one and we are all one.

Journey Through the Chakras: Higher Self Chakra

Colour	Gold
Location	Above the Crown to the back of the head
Qualities and Functions of the Higher Self Chakra	The Higher Self Chakra, also referred to as the Soul Star Chakra, is your connection to your soul self; your Higher Self, your first point of connection to divinity. This chakra is your connection to higher knowledge, the akasha, past lives and your connection to source. Through this chakra, you connect to your Higher Self and bring through knowledge that best serves you. You will be given what you are ready for. Mastery is embodying more of your Higher Self and living as your Higher Self. Your Higher Self is the source of perfect health, instant manifestation, inner knowing and higher wisdom.
	When activated you realise yourself as a spiritual being, a divine soul. Divine light then flows through you, replenishing your entire being, empowering, informing and enlightening you. The full essence and power of your accumulated soul experiences are available here. Accessing the akashic records (the universal ethernet where everything is recorded and written up) is possible from within your Soul Star Chakra as is total soul realisation.
Key Functions for Mastery	• Mastering the Laws of Meditation and Oneness. • Mastering the gifts of your higher mind. • Being your true higher self masterfully.

Mastery is being your Self, living as your Self, and being true to your True Self

The Nature of the Higher Conscious Mind

- Your higher conscious mind, also called your Higher Self or Guardian Spirit, is the Divine in you; your connection to the higher realms. Your Higher Self is the eternal you that has always existed; the real you that goes beyond time and space; beyond past and future.

- Your Higher Self is beyond gender – balanced male and female energy.

- Connection and communication with your Higher Self can make everything right for you. Your Higher Self has the ability to recognise causes; the source of events which is a key factor in healing. Your Higher Self has the power to know, predict and effect the future. Your future is not cast in stone and has multiple potential outcomes. You always have free will. Your Higher Self has knowledge of your life purpose and can guide you on your path. Your Higher Self has insight in the entire universe and is the source of your intuition and inspiration.

- Extra-sensory perception (ESP) is a function of your higher mind so your Higher Self has the power to produce attainments such as clairvoyance, clairaudience, inner knowing, intuition, telepathy and distant healing.

- Your Higher Self sees you as perfect, sees everyone else as perfect and sees your life in perfect order. Operating as your Higher Self means you are free from mistakes. Your Higher Self is beyond judgement and all-forgiving because it sees all as one. Your Higher Self is beyond conscious description, beyond language and can only be experienced through your Unconscious Mind, your intuitive self.

- Your Higher Self is the source of manifestation. It has the blueprint of perfect health, so approaching your Higher Self can bring about instant healing. It has the power to remove (uncreate) anything that negatively impacts you, such as physical and psychological disease, complexes, emotions, fixations and false identification, and can do so instantaneously (Long, 1953).

- Your Higher Self respects the Conscious Mind's free will and therefore must be asked. It wants for you only to have peace and always gives you what you ask for.

- In the process of evolution, the Higher Self represents who you are becoming.

Mastery is coming home to yourself

Connection with Your Higher Self

Reality is created from consciousness. As you increase and expand your consciousness, your reality changes radically and dimensionally. By raising your vibrations and connecting with your Higher Self, you expand your consciousness.

The higher the levels of your energy vibratory frequencies (as illustrated in the ladder of emotional levels in Step 2) the closer you are to your Higher Self. For close connection, your Higher Self wants you to be free from past negative emotions, limiting beliefs, false identifications and energy-draining connections.

Connection with your Higher Self gives you access to inner knowing, higher wisdom and increases manifestation capability. This connection restores peace, good health and youthfulness. Ultimately, we heal by connecting with our soul.

Your Unconscious Mind holds the keys to connection with your Higher Self. We can't consciously conceive of the Higher Self. Communication is channelled through your unconscious mind in symbolic language, visualisation, feelings, sensations in the body, gut-feel and the like (as illustrated in Step 3 Figure 3).

Mastery is knowing thyself

The Path of Personal Evolution

The path of growth and development through the chakras to higher levels of awareness is also a path of growth from physical to emotional, then mental and finally spiritual. Carl Jung said, like the (true Higher) Self, we have the unconscious mind from birth, out of which the conscious mind emerges in the course of childhood development. Developing a strong and effective ego is important to function in the outer world. Our advance work in developing a healthy ego is to bring more and more of our unconscious habits and patterns into conscious awareness. Eventually we reach a stage when we realise that our true Higher Self is more real and more true than the ego. At this stage we begin the work of integrating the minds into one and eventually we may begin to attain higher consciousness (Snowden, 2010).

To know who you are becoming, familiarise yourself with the qualities of your Higher Self. This is a paradox as you are already who you are becoming. It is more a homecoming to yourself; a fulfilment of who you truly are. To further your personal evolution, begin to operate more from the level of your Higher Self. This work will expose the illusion of the ego further. We don't fight the ego, rather we integrate it. You only have to recognise the ego and then have the intention to surrender the ego to the Higher Self. Then see the Higher Self embracing the ego and bringing it in, into oneness. This is a powerful visualisation that can be incorporated into a meditation. Integrating the minds into one, brings us into wholeness. The word whole is the root and true meaning of health, holy, holistic and healing. When we achieve this wholeness, and we know we are all one, the ego judgements, projections and reactions stop. When you realise that what you react to in others is also in you, the ego is exposed, and you stop seeing yourself as a victim (Tolle, 2005). Instead of projecting, you are now free to extend yourself, your true light, and your service in this world.

The Essence of Enlightenment

When you raise your consciousness into your Higher Self and operate as your Higher Self:

- You are free from fear, truly fearless.
- You feel unconditional love for all things and everyone.
- You have access to true wisdom – all-knowing, all-seeing.
- You are all-powerful, yet humble – something the ego is incapable of.
- You are all-forgiving, all-accepting.

- You are beyond judgement; beyond the duality of right and wrong, good and bad, everything is just an experience.
- You are free from attachments to outcomes and personal investments.
- You are mindful; flowing in the moment.
- You experience peace, joy and bliss.
- Your life is more about being than doing.
- You are of one mind – integrated, whole and aligned.
- Instant healing is possible.
- Instant manifestation is achievable.
- You can control your thoughts and communicate telepathically.
- You don't fix things (nothing is damaged) you just create another reality – of perfection.

Mastery is acting powerfully whilst remaining humble

Table 3: Your Evolution from Ego to Higher Self

Ego Mind	Higher Mind
Head	Heart
Fear	Love
Stress	Peace and Joy
Blame	Compassion
Judgement	Forgiveness
Duality, division, separation	Interconnectedness, oneness
Scarcity	Abundance
Selfishness	Generosity
Arrogance	True Power
Control	Creative, wise
Doing	Being
Limiting beliefs	Infinite potential
Anger, frustration, guilt	Kindness, patience, freedom
Disease	Health
Force	Flow
Resistant	Expansive
Concrete	Abstract

The Mastermind-set

- I am whole.
- I am divine love.
- I am divine light.

Mastery Practices

- Be your masterful True Self.
- Be light-hearted.
- Practise compassion.
- Judge nothing, accept what is.
- Remain the observer.
- Practise heart-based consciousness.
- Tune into and honour your inner guidance.
- Own and embrace you power.
- Be the change, the healer, the teacher, the way-maker, the light-bearer.

Integrate the Ego

Continue to recognise the ego and bring it into wholeness by surrendering ego to your Higher Self. See and feel your Higher Self embracing the ego and your minds becoming one. Move into unity in yourself first and then be one with the universe.

Heighten Your Inner Knowing

You can communicate and get guidance from your Higher Self with a yes/no signal.

How to Get a Yes/No Signal

Agree a signal with your Higher Self:

- It may be an image of your Higher Self lifting a left or right arm.

- It may be a light flash in your inner vision either on the right or the left side.
- You may feel an energy sensation, like a pulsation or tingling, either on the left or right side of your body.
- It may be that you are physically pulled more to the left or the right side of your body.
- You can also just get a feeling that it is right.
- You can use your body as a pendulum. The body may be swaying forward for a yes or backward for a no.
- You can dowse using a pendulum.

Meditation

Connecting with Your Higher Self
- Start every day by connecting with your Higher Self.
- Do so by sitting in a meditative state.
- Ground, protect, connect.
- Visualise the light of your Higher Self like a golden ball of light above you.
- Bring it down as a column of light into your body.
- Fill yourself with the nourishing, uplifting energy of your Higher Self.
- Connect with your Higher Self. Sense the energy sensations.
- Sit in the energies of love, joy and peace.
- Meditate on the Higher Self, your source of higher knowledge.
- Communicate with the Higher Self and ask any questions regarding your own true purpose and path.
- Ground the energy in and set the intention to live your day as your Higher Self.
- This practice over time activates the gifts of your higher mind.

Visit
www.brightfuturenow.co.uk/meditations
to download or listen to a free audio meditation:
Connecting with your Higher Self

Step 12: Master Universal Consciousness

We used to live cut off, practically quarantined, fallen into a 3-dimensional density. With the higher consciousness grid activated now, we are connected in again as true multi-dimensional beings, able to access universal, cosmic and divine consciousness once again.

Journey Through the Chakras: Divine Consciousness Chakra

Colour	Pearlescent – White light with rainbow light
Location	Above the Crown and Higher Self Chakra
Qualities and Functions of the Divine Consciousness Chakra	This chakra is about connecting with spirit, the divine, the creator of all. It also promotes universal consciousness, our connection with the higher consciousness energy grid and all that is infinite.
	Located above the Higher Self Chakra, the Divine Consciousness Chakra is a portal; a doorway to the higher realms, to source light, the universe and the wider cosmos.
	When activated, divine light can then freely pour in through your Soul Star Chakra, down your spinal column and all your chakras, through your Earth Star Chakra, and connect to the light at the core of the Earth. You then become a perfect channel of light. This chakra has the qualities of interconnectedness, oneness, community, moving beyond the individual self and becoming part of the whole, working as a collective.
Key Functions for Mastery	• Mastering Universal Laws and concepts of Time, Space, Interconnectedness/Oneness. • Mastering connection with source. • Mastering universal consciousness.

Master the Key Universal Laws of Time, Space, Energy

- *The Law of Time*: The only moment we have is now. This is where we create. What we have done is done. The future only happens in and from the present tense and is built of today's thoughts, dressed by emotions and driven by action.
- *The Law of the Present Moment*: Time doesn't exist. What we refer to as past and future have no reality except in our own mental constructs. The idea of time is a convention of thought and language, a social agreement. In truth, we only have the Present Moment.
- *The Law of Unity*: We are all One.
- *The Laws of Interconnectedness/Oneness*: Everything is connected and of the same essence.
- *Law of Faith*: Believe and you will receive. When you have faith in the Divine, you know that whatever the outcome, will be for the highest and greatest good of all.
- *The Law of Grace*: Supersedes the Law of Karma. We can invoke the Law of Grace, provided we've learnt our lessons. Give grace to receive grace.

Moving Beyond Time and Space

Mastering time is an essential practice. We live in a fast-paced world, where a lot has to be crammed in and time never seems enough. The master lives in a world of abundance and infinity – it is the same with time. How do we overcome the perceived limitations of time and space in an ever-busy and stressful world?

To master time, we have to let go of our three-dimensional concept of linear time – that one event follows the next, creating past, present and future. Non-linear time may be circular, quantum, even holographic – everything happening at the same time, concurrently. Carl Jung (Snowden, 2010) described non-linear time as synchronicity, the basis of coincidences. Events seem to be connected in a quantum way rather than a linear way. In a holographic universe, the past can spill over into the present through what we may call déjà vu. We can change events that have already happened, something we often do in Transformational Therapy to heal emotions and trauma. Equally, the future being malleable, can reach back into the present through synchronised events. You may stumble upon vital information for a key project, or by coincidence or chance bump into someone who later turns out to be your soulmate or future business partner. Many people shared their stories about how they were prevented from going to work on the day of 9/11, the Twin Towers disaster in the USA, and on 7/7, during the London bombings. Something that may seem like a mishap – an illness or missing the train – that later saved their lives. The master is more interested in the purpose and meaning of events, rather than in their causes, knowing everything happens for a reason. This makes us more accepting of how events turn out, trusting in the bigger scheme of things. Instead of trying to force things in a three-dimensional way, battling away against the clock, let go and flow with life.

To overcome time is to overcome the searching, the pressure of ego desire for achievement and becoming, and realise that we are already what we search for. We are already where we want to be. When we stop searching and striving, then time no longer has any meaning and stops. Then we can enter the magic of the time-expanding moment of Now.

By means of your fifth-dimensional tools of intention-setting and visualisation, you step outside of time into the timeless quantum world of energy. With your mind you reach into the future to envision future outcomes. As a creator you utilise the minimum of time and energy because you elicit the might of the universe and its infinity of resources, time and space to conspire on your behalf. Things will then fall in place for you effortlessly, as the universe rearranges things through people and circumstances in ways you could not have imagined. Living in the timeless present moment means you expand time. You can access more of your creative resources and get more done in less time.

Mastery is Surrendering into the One Mind

At the higher levels of consciousness, the laws and concepts of how the universe works become paradoxical. At the level of the conscious mind, we want to resolve paradoxes to establish which are true and which not. The master is able to hold two or more seemingly contradictory principles in his mind at the same time. As an example, there is nothing to be fearful of. At some level of three-dimensional reality, fear may be real like in a war zone or area of high crime. At a fifth-dimensional level of consciousness, you are beyond fear. You are eternal therefore always safe. When you emanate loving vibrations, you attract more love and positivity to you. Another example is that you are a small cog in a big wheel of the universe. At the same time, you are the universe. The grass is in the seed and the seed is in the grass.

Mastery is flowing with Spirit

Universal Consciousness

Expanded consciousness first takes us beyond the ego and its focus on the material world. As we continue to seek the truth, we may move in and out of belief systems. This can be helpful at stages as there is wisdom to be found in any belief system. Belief systems are essentially exclusive, invested in their own perception of right and wrong, and therefore limiting. Respect the beauty of diversity, embrace the wisdom that can be found and transcend the belief systems. Mastery is staying open to new learning, new ways of seeing things, not holding onto any perception of truth. Move beyond the illusions of separation, differences and all the divisions the human mind has created and rediscover our commonality, our original wholeness, the truth of our true authentic original selves. Become a true ambassador of unity and peace and experience the freedom of all-embracing universal consciousness.

The universe goes beyond life on Earth, perhaps beyond life in our universe. With the discovery of thousands of exoplanets orbiting other stars, the search for life elsewhere has entered an exciting new phase. Scientists are now also exploring the concept of multiverses.

Is Our Universe Just One of Many?

Seth Shostak directs the search for extra-terrestrials at the SETI Institute in California. In looking for evidence of intelligent life in space, scientists ponder the idea of life in parallel universes. The idea of parallel universes isn't new. You find it in many fields of thought. But, in the physics community, the debate about this concept has heated up in recent years. New research has suggested that the Big Bang may have been only one of countless others, that parallel universes might exist. As Shostak explains: 'The idea that other universes might exist arises from the realisation that the Big Bang might not have been a unique event but a common one' (Shostak, n.d.).

The possibility of an almost infinite number of universes – some inhabited – is mind-blowing. There is always more to discover. Our consciousness is ever-expanding.

The Higher Realms

The Universe is created by thought and we are miniature versions of the universe. In the same way we create our reality with emotionally powerful thoughts (Talbot, 1991).

Creativity, imagination, awareness and spirituality is situated in the implicate (the energy field). The future as a hologram is substantive enough for us to perceive it, yet malleable enough to be susceptible to change. The future is fluid and composed of crystallising possibilities. The consciousness plays a significant role in creating the here and now and in literally sculpting our own destiny. In *The Holographic Universe* (1991), Michael Talbot describes the higher realms (the implicate, void, thought-built reality, land where spirits dwell, afterlife, the archetypal source from which all earthly forms originate and will return) from extensive research with people who have had near death (ND) experiences. Similar themes ran through the reported ND experiences:

- An experience of a tunnel, light and reception by deceased relatives into a splendorous light-filled realm where time and space does not exist.
- Encounters with beings of light and a life review in which beings of light assisted gently and non-coercively.
- Life review is a vivid recall of their entire life, all happening in an instant – like a three-dimensional movie whilst experiencing all the accompanying emotions of their own and others involved. Every thought is relived. It is like simultaneously experiencing the whole and every part.
- They are never judged by the beings of light – they act as guides and counsellors whose only purpose is to teach. They feel only love and acceptance in their presence.
- The only judgement is self-judgement as a result of introspection.
- A total lack of cosmic judgement or divine system of punishment and rewards is most often reported as the most controversial aspect.
- The universe is far more benevolent/compassionate than we think.
- Only two things that are really important: love and knowledge.

- There is no right or wrong. The only moral criteria: did you do it out of love? Was love your motivation? Did you learn from it?
- A key message was to learn to love more. Replace anger with love; learn to forgive; love everyone unconditionally. Learn that we in turn are loved.
- We are placed on earth to learn that love is key.
- Instant knowledge prevails in the afterlife – access to all knowledge is instant.
- Physical bodies revert to whole, perfect, younger versions or are shaped by thought. We are also composed of colour frequencies, of light and we are also constituted out of sound. Each person has his own musical tone range and colour range.
- The ability to see in all directions at once.
- Things like food are created by thought – no need to eat but you can if you wish to.
- Information takes the place of food as a source of nourishment.
- It is a world composed of various subtle vibrations of colour and light, endless in size, infinitely more beautiful, with forests, mountains and beautiful cities of staggering architectural designs, opal lakes, bright seas, rainbow rivers and institutions of higher learning literally built out of knowledge.
- Communication is telepathic, through 'light pictures'.
- A single thought can materialise whole gardens with fragrant flowers. In a way heaven is thought-built, especially through coordinated thought.
- The explicate may not be all that different from the implicate – thought can manifest, it just takes a little more time.
- Beings of light are entities who have completed their cycle of reincarnation here.
- They radiate love, compassion, warmth and friendliness that evoke complete trust.

- From the beings themselves light streams outward in every direction, leaving those in contact with the effect of extraordinary lightness, joy and ecstasy.
- It is a world of seamlessness, whole, interconnectedness of all things – no separateness. It is only as one descends from higher vibrational levels of reality to the lower that a progressive law of fragmentation takes over. We fragment things because we exist at a lower vibration of consciousness and reality. It is our tendency to fragment that keeps us from experiencing the intensity of joy, love and delight that is the norm in these higher and more subtle realms.
- This wholeness also points to ultimate relativity of all truths (no rights and wrongs) and that any attempt to reduce the universe to absolute facts and doctrine leads to distortion and separateness. Therefore, we must go beyond organised religion, seeking true spirituality.
- As above so below: the without is like the within; the small is like the large; what is here is elsewhere.
- There are different planes of consciousness and many higher planes.
- The purpose of life is to learn and evolve.
- Heaven is the archetypal source from which all earthly forms originate, by which they are nourished, and to which all forms ultimately return.

The Mastermind-set

- We are all one.
- I am one with the universe.
- There is only this moment of now.
- As the Earth shifts in evolution, the universe shifts.
- We are all on a path of ascension.
- As I do my inner work, the outer world responds.

Mastery Practices

Connect In

Ground through the Earth Star Chakra to connect into the fifth-dimensional consciousness grid, as described in Step 8. This is a quick, safe and powerful way of connecting with the higher realms. Bring love and light to the world by being a column of pure white light. Send this light into the Earth for earth healing. Intend that this light allows your invisible helpers, angels and light beings to enter to assist with certain tasks or to uplift the whole. With thought-intention (and respect for free will) send light to people and places for healing and upliftment.

Continued Purification

Continue your purification by identifying and releasing any negative thoughts and negative emotions. As you do, you can let in more light. When the light of your aura is clear and bright, you are kept safe, protected and uplifted in the light.

Blessing

Practise the gift of blessing. It invokes divine energy. What you give you receive.

Detached Awareness

Practise awareness of the illusionary aspects of the three-dimensional world. Remain the detached observer. Be in the world but not of the world. Live the values of your higher mind. Use the gifts of your higher mind.

The Path of Spiritual Maturity

When we are spiritually immature, we are very much faced with the three-dimensional world and the troubles we experience. We can feel a victim in an unfair world, blaming and pointing fingers. We pray to a source outside of us, asking for help.

As we mature more into our own empowerment, discovering the power of our own mind, our own ability to respond, we may use affirmations to imprint positive beliefs on our Unconscious Mind – a more fourth-dimensional way of creating desired outcomes.

Your awareness expands, and you become conscious of the interconnectedness of everything. You begin to yield to a higher power and flow more with your inner guidance. As a channel of divine love and light, you wonder what the universe wants to do through you today.

You Are It

As you step into the mastership of higher consciousness, you realise that you are it. That there is no one outside of you that isn't you. That you are a creator. You align yourself with Spirit and merge with the quantum pool of energy, vibration and light. You imprint your vision on the aether. Your will and higher will become one. As a master your effect on the world is great. You have more power than you know. It's your gift, your responsibility and your calling to co-create the world you want to live in.

You Are a Creator

The master commands, co-creates and accepts the responsibility that goes with that. The master creates only for the highest and greatest good of all. The master takes charge, makes decisions and accepts complete mastery of his/her life. As a master you know you are the creator of your own reality; the master of your own destiny. When you imprint your thought-intention into the aether, the whole universe rearranges itself to bring about what you command. Do this with integrity, powerfully and humbly, in service of the whole.

This is the greatest time ever to be alive

Multi-Dimensional Mastery

Recent research describes the brain as being made up of multi-dimensional geometrical structures and spaces. They found that neural networks form structures with up to eleven dimensions. Ran Levi from Aberdeen University who worked on the research paper explains: 'It is as if the brain reacts to a stimulus by building then razing a tower of multi-dimensional blocks, starting with rods (1D), then planks (2D), then cubes (3D), and then more complex geometries with 4D, 5D, etc. The progression of activity through the brain resembles a multi-dimensional sandcastle that materialises out of the sand and then disintegrates' (Beall, 2017).

We are multi-dimensional beings. As a master you are from the higher planes, incarnated here to do great work. Mastery is having the insight into the nature of existence on the different planes and having the flexibility; the flux and flow to move your consciousness; your awareness in and out of dimensions, for the purpose of assisting others. There are many dimensions, each with sub-dimensions. These dimensions relate to our minds and subtle bodies and so you actually exist energetically in multiple dimensions as you can see from Table 4 below.

Table 4: Multi-Dimensional Consciousness

Planes	Minds	Levels of Consciousness
Spiritual plane	Infinite One Mind	Upper: infinite perfection
	Higher Self	Lower: higher consciousness
Mental plane	Conscious Mind	Upper: abstract thoughts, ideas, aspirations
	Conscious Mind	Lower: concrete thinking
Astral plane	Unconscious Mind	Upper: emotions, imagination
Etherical plane	Unconscious Mind	Lower: urges, desires
Physical plane	Physical Body	Form, matter

It's not always easy for us to grasp higher levels of consciousness from the level of our everyday consciousness. David Roberts, author of *12 Dimensions of Consciousness and Beyond* (2018) gives us an unusually clear understanding of what may be postulated as 12 levels of consciousness. I've summarised his fascinating work in Table 5 below.

Table 5: 12 Dimensional Consciousness

Dimensions	Description	Evolution of Consciousness	Our Creative Experiences
First	Where we experience time	Consciousness	Our experiences
Second	Space-time	Awareness	Differentiation Interpretation Illusion
Third	Space-time-gravity	Identity Ourselves as three in one mind	Matter Events become our Reality Past, present, future
Fourth	Many worlds Many realities Many versions of me	Many versions Multiverses Many outcomes Many lifetimes Our dream world	Possibility Many possibilities
Fifth	Beyond time Spirit world	From where we choose to enter into time, and where we go when we leave here	Choice We have powerful choice Choice manifests
Sixth	Creator dimension of me	Creator consciousness	Using thought to create Thought manifests

Seventh	Many creators	We are the many creators	Desire manifests
Eighth	Multiverse	Many universes Parallel universes	
Ninth	All that is	Everything that exists	
Tenth	The impossible becomes possible		
Eleventh	Beyond possibility		
Twelfth	Prime creator of everything		
Thirteenth?	Many prime creators?		

David Roberts describe our creative process as our seventh-dimensional self having a desire, that creates thought (6d) with which we choose (5d) from many possibilities (4d) to create our events (3d) that are the (illusionary) interpretations (2d) of our experiences (1d), as set out in the last column of the table above.

Everything that you have created in your life and the current reality you are experiencing, first comes from your inner reality. It is the result of your thoughts, feelings, emotions, energy and consciousness. Your inner world creates your outer world.

While the nervous system is designed to give you what you focus on, we can and do create from the level of the ego mind. Yet, you are more than that and operate creatively at different dimensions. When you go into the stillness through meditation, you access higher dimensions. Your awareness can then expand to take in the bigger picture and the wisdom of a higher perspective. This higher perspective you can bring to your everyday happening, seeing the synchronicity and the deeper meaning in the ordinary, even challenging experiences.

The master understands the illusionary nature of life on the three-dimensional material world of form. The master also understands that, even though we are not from this world, we are living in this world and have to see to our physical needs and comforts. Even though it is illusionary, it is 'a reality' where many reside in consciousness. Whilst you maintain a detached higher vision of the three-dimensional world and its work-, family- and finance-related strains and stresses, true mastery is also having the compassion for anyone experiencing these three-dimensional challenges. We are all on various stages of our path of evolution. Some may even have gone back a few steps to pick up essential experiences. Judge no one. Hold the high vibrational light for everyone.

Multi-dimensional awareness also means you can look at perceptions and projections from a higher level, bringing the essential learning, insights and perspectives into your awareness. As you continue to integrate these insights and grow, you eventually move beyond the need for projection. When all of your shadow has been brought into the light and dissolved, projection stops. Then you are free to extend yourself and your service in the world (Tolle, 2005).

Creating from a Higher Reality

When you bring yourself in alignment with the field of universal intelligence and the divine mind, you are more likely to create what is for your own greater good, the greater good of others and the planet as a whole. When you are in alignment with the whole, what you want will manifest so much more quickly and you can fast-track your results in life.

You are multi-dimensional and when you create in alignment with your purpose, you create masterfully. What you want, then, will be in alignment with what wants to flow through you.

Accessing Divine Mind Synergy

Divine mind synergy is the ability to open up to the ever present and all-encompassing universal intelligence, receiving pure inspiration, guidance and wisdom. Divine mind synergy allows you to move out of the thinking mind and the intellectual experiences and biases of the ego mind, and obtain an expanded view of any given situation, taking into account all positions and not just your own. This way you access an intelligence that is an all-encompassing view of humanity and sees the most magnificent picture and highest potential in all situations and circumstances for the greatest good of all. It takes a shift into the vibration of love to unlock divine mind synergy. The gateway is through the heart. Love is the gateway to this universal intelligence and flowing it through you. This is often described as a state flow.

From a place of peace and stillness, enter the void where there is no thought, no agenda and all of creation is possible. Here your consciousness is connected with the consciousness of the creator of all. The illusionary veils of separation are dissolved so you can unite your mind with all there is and tap into the infinite creative power. Then you can examine things from a higher perspective. From this place of connection, magic happens. As you enter divine mind synergy, the unique expression of your divine gifts will materialise.

In divine mind synergy, you find yourself operating more as part of a group consciousness. You can access the quantum field easily. Here you can merge with lightworkers across the world, to create in synergy. This is the divine mind synergy in action. Entering into this state allows telepathic communication, synchronicity and effortless manifestation. It can often be seen in nature, for example, ants or bees all working together telepathically as one hive mind, serving the whole.

To access divine mind synergy, be clear of mind, free from ego thoughts and pure of heart, with the intention to serve your purpose, for the greater good of all.

In *Star Wars, The Last Jedi*, Luke Skywalker teaches Rey about the Force. He says the Force is the energy that holds all things together, ensures balance and binds the universe together. It's all around you and also inside you. He teaches her how to get in touch with the Force: Breathe and reach out with your feelings. Open up to perceive the subtle teachings of truth.

Meditation

Divine Mind Synergy
- Ground, protect, connect.
- Visualise the light of the Higher Self like a golden bubble of light above you.
- Bring it down as a column of light into your body.
- Fill yourself with the nourishing, uplifting energy of your Higher Self.
- Bring your awareness to the Sacred Heart, the gateway.
- Set the intention to connect with source, the divine creator.
- Receive the wisdom teachings.
- Align with the divine love and light.
- Tap into the creative power.
- Create the New Earth and your role in it.

Visit
www.brightfuturenow.co.uk/meditations
to download or listen to a free audio meditation:
Divine Mind Synergy

***

Elemental Breath Meditation – an Ancient Sufi Practice

Twenty-Five Breaths to Change Consciousness

- First 5 breaths, EARTH
  - Breathe in and out through the mouth.
  - As you breathe, reaffirm your connection to the Earth, the solid support that your body provides and your place in that body on the planet. Be aware of the connection through your DNA to the ancient ancestors that have lived upon the Earth. A lineage of life upon this planet. You are part of that history. Relax your body and let the Earth support you.
- Second 5 breaths, WATER
  - Breathe in through the nose and out through the mouth. As you breathe visualise a waterfall flowing down from the top of your head, through your body and into the earth. This water is washing away impurities and balancing the emotions. Allow your being to become more fluid and less solid. The water of life is flowing through you and connects you to all the water on the planet.
- Third 5 breaths, FIRE
  - Breathe in through the mouth and out through the nose. As you breathe IN feel the warmth of the fire breath in your belly (solar plexus). This is the fire of transformation. Breathe OUT gently at the heart centre sending light out in all directions. The soft breath of light expands around you transforming the fire energy into the light of love and compassion. This is the higher energy of the fire element and links to spiritual growth.

- Fourth 5 breaths, AIR
  - Breathe gently in and out through the mouth. Feel the lightness of the air element filling your body. The whole body expanding with the air element. Lighter and lighter creating more space within. Be aware that this same breath has been breathed by generations of people. It is transforming you and the planet.
- Fifth 5 breaths, ETHER
  - Breathe even more gently in through the nose and out through the nose. This gentle breath brings the lightness and spaciousness of the ether element. Your whole being is now less substantial, spaciousness created inside and around you.
  - Sit with this feeling of spaciousness for a few moments before getting on with your day. Feel at one with the Universe. Knowing that this too, is your existence.

Contributed by Sue Keady, Tai Chi Teacher

***

Epilogue

A Journey Completed

We've been on an exceptional journey of evolution. It's been a journey of advanced healing, growth and personal expansion. We've moved beyond an old stress-creating world view of materialism, separation, conflict and exploitation.

Opening Up to the Magic of Life

As the mind finally shifts out of its fear-based, ego-based consciousness, we begin to open up to a whole new magical realm of positivity, joy and creativity – a new realm of infinite potential where anything is possible. Fear has many opposites such as hope, faith and trust. The true opposite of fear is love. When the fear goes you can access the power of love and positivity and open up to your true potential.

As your life begins to turn more positive and brighter, you will progressively feel lighter and more free. As the old paradigm crumbles, you begin to see clearly. You are now aware of a reality where you are the creator of your own outcomes. You may begin to experience the magical synchronicity of events in your life – people and experiences are drawn to you by the power of positive, loving, creative thoughts and intentions. A subtle, guiding, intuitive voice, steers you along a purposeful path. As you flow more in the moment with the magic that life has installed for you, things begin to fall in place for you – sometimes in ways you couldn't imagine yourself. With the old fears and stresses gone, youthfulness and good health returns. The more you shift into a relaxed, creative mode of being, the more you reclaim your potential. With the old limiting perceptions gone, you begin to unfold as your true magnificent self. Your universe begins to take on a new nature; one of expansion, abundance, infinite possibility and pure potential. Now you are free from the ordinary; free to create the extraordinary from a place of love, joy, growth, imagination, inspiration, power and purpose.

The Journey is Ongoing

Mastery is ongoing practice

- *Continue* to make meditation your daily discipline. Through meditation you stay connected, receive your inner guidance and recharge yourself with the nourishing, uplifting light of enlightenment.
- *Continue* your energy practices through which you take charge of your own health and grow the light bodies as your vehicle for ascension.
- *Continue* your healing. Old habits and unresolved issues will continue to surface. Recognise that they come up to heal. Reflect on them, learn and release the old so you can accommodate more love and light.
- *Continue* to create. Mastery is the magic of creating change in your external environment by making wilful changes in yourself.
- *Continue* to grow in your understanding and application of the Spiritual Laws. Let the Laws guide you as you flow with

spirit, create purposefully and become more joyful, loving and light-filled. By living the Laws, you will grow in mastery as you serve humanity by establishing heaven on earth. Life becomes more harmonious, peaceful and purposeful. This is a time of a shift in consciousness on Earth, it holds an unprecedented opportunity for spiritual growth. It is an exciting time of immense change and infinite possibilities. We don't know what the future holds. It's easy to look at the state of the world and wonder what will happen. The master is not led by external factors. It's our role to create the New Earth. The Laws will guide you in your growth and offer you a new clarity of your role in furthering the collective quantum leap in consciousness, whilst dreaming the new era of enlightenment into existence.

- **Continue** to embrace your power. Reveal who you truly are. Now is not a time to contract, hide, withdraw or clash. Now is the time to be supportive, generous, expansive, creative and loving. You have been through immense transformation. Now is a time to unveil the new you. Now is a time to BE the new paradigm, not longing for it, hoping for it or waiting for it. Make it happen now. Create the new paradigm with your own behaviour. Now is the time to shine. The New Era is here. This is the start of the New Age of Aquarius; the age of peace, harmony and oneness. It is time to be your most powerful, masterful, magnificent, wise and gifted self. This is our time. This is what we incarnated for.

A new world awaits, step into it powerfully

Envisioning a New World

I have a vision of a new golden era on Earth
Where all people live in respect, acceptance, compassion and
love for each other
Where everyone feels free to develop their true unique talents
creatively for the greater good
Where we learn and grow in unity, positivity, curiosity,
excitement and love
Where everyone does what they love, what makes them happy,
serving the whole joyfully

I see a world of fairness, equality, community, support and
harmony
People living in close connection with the Earth and its natural
cycles once again
Nature is honoured and all creatures respected and treated with
kindness
Plants and trees flourish abundantly as we work the land with
love and gratitude again
Good health and youthfulness – our natural state – returns

*New inventions spring up, new means of travel, environment-
friendly energy sources abound
Communities flourishing abundantly, joyfully cooperating,
sharing, supporting, caring for all
Children are free to be, to learn to explore in their own
wonderful way
Our hearts open, synchronising our inner-tuition, making
decisions for the good of all
The magic of life is felt everywhere
Humans walk with angels again
Communicating with our brethren of other planets again
Love, joy, peace and brightest light await
Thanks to you who co-create
The new golden era on a magnificent New Earth*

Resources for Your Transformation

There is always more to learn and discover as we continue to grow and evolve in consciousness. Visit www.foundationsofmastery.com where you can enjoy ongoing access to the audio meditations. Stay in touch. Subscribe to our newsletter at www.brightfuturenow.co.uk and keep up to date with the latest developments, products, courses, workshops and talks.

Chakra Activation

Accelerate your evolution with our healing sessions, in person or online, aimed at addressing specific issues and activating your chakras, whether the seven main chakras or the new Sacred Chakras. These powerful healing and activation sessions also activate your DNA and open you up to your higher gifts. More details about these and more courses, as well as the opportunity to book sessions can be found on our website: www.brightfuturenow.co.uk.

Healing and Transformational Meditations

Enjoy ongoing access to the audio versions of the powerful healing and transformational meditations in this book. Visit www.foundationsofmastery.com to listen to the meditations and facilitate your own healing and growth at any time.

Soul Coaching

Join our signature Soul Coaching programme – in person or online wherever you are in the world. Take your transformation and evolution to another level, grow in enlightenment and live purposefully. More details and booking facilities can be found on the website: www.brightfuturenow.co.uk.

Transformational Therapy

This is the quickest and most powerful way to clear up all your karma so you can evolve in enlightenment and ascension. Experience a complete clear-out, heal and release all negative emotions and baggage from the past – anger, sadness, fear, hurt and guilt. Also let go of limiting beliefs that keep you from reaching your highest potential, and develop empowering beliefs instead. More details and booking facilities can be found on: www.brightfuturenow.co.uk.

***

Also by the Author

Lifting the Veils of Illusion, 7 Steps to Spiritual Enlightenment facilitates an all-encompassing journey of personal empowerment and spiritual growth in seven essential steps. Taking a peek into the unseen, sharing ancient wisdom and consulting ground-breaking science, you will gain fascinating new insights and experience powerful transformational shifts – from stress and fear to true empowerment. Set out in seven Key Steps, this book is not only massively informative, packed with wisdom, it's also hugely transformational as it contains the healing techniques that the author has been using to magical effect in her therapy, coaching and courses. In one book you have a complete guide to navigating the path of healing and spiritual enlightenment. In addition, there is a fascinating glimpse of the New Era, as predicted by the ancients, that we are entering here now on Earth.

Resource List

Beall, Abigail. 'The multi-dimensional universe hiding inside your head', *Wired*, 12 June, www.wired.co.uk/article/neurons-multi-dimensional-network-brains (2017)

Beckwith, Michael Bernard. *The Life Visioning Process* (2008)

Benedict, Gerald. *The Mayan Prophesies for 2012* (2008)

Cannon, Dolores. *The Three Waves of Volunteers and the New Earth* (2011)

Chia, Mantak and Joyce Thom. *Craniosacral Chi Kung: Integrating Body and Emotion in the Cosmic Flow* (2016)

Chia, Mantak and Juan Li. *The Inner Structure of Tai Chi* (1996)

Chopra, Deepak. *Seven Spiritual Laws of Success* (1994)

Chopra, Deepak. *Syncrodestiny* (2003)

Cooper, Diane. *A Little Light on the Spiritual Laws* (2000)

Dalai Lama and Desmond Tutu. *The Book of Joy* (2016)

Dannelley, Richard. *Sedona: Beyond the Vortex* (1995)

Dupree, Ulrich. *Ho'oponopono* (2012)

Dyer, Wayne W. *You'll See It When You Believe It: The Way to Your Personal Transformation* (1989)

Eden, Donna. *Energy Medicine* (1998)

Edwards, Gill. *Consciousness Medicine* (2010)

Edwards, Lonnie C. *Spiritual Laws That Govern Humanity and the Universe* (2015)

Emoto, Masaru. *The Hidden Messages in Water* (2004)

Foundation for Inner Peace. *A Course in Miracles* (1992)

Frankl, Viktor E. *Man's Search for Meaning* (2013)

Hanson, Rick. *Buddah's Brain* (2009)

Hawkins, David R. *Power vs. Force: The Hidden Determinants of Human Behaviour* (1995)

Hay, Louise. *You Can Heal Your Life* (1984)

Heaversedge, Jonty and Ed Halliwell. *The Mindfulness Manifesto: How Doing Less and Noticing More Can Help Us Thrive in a Stressed-out World* (2010)

James, Tad. *Hypnosis, a Comprehensive Guide* (2000)

Judith, Anodea. *Chakras: Wheels of Life* (2004)

King, Serge K. *Ancient Hawaiian Secrets for Modern Living* (2008)

Kornfield, Jack. *A Path with Heart* (2002)

Lipton, Bruce H. *The Biology of Beliefs* (2005)

Long, Max Freedom. *The Secret Science at Work: New Light on Prayer* (1953)

Millman, Dan. *The Life you were Born to Live, a Guide to Finding your Life Purpose* (1993)

Myss, Caroline. *Anatomy of Spirit* (1996)

Ober, Clinton, Stephen Sinatra and Martin Zucker. *Earthing: The Most Important Health Discovery Ever* (2010)

Perlmutter, David and Alberto Villoldo. *Power Up Your Brain, the Neuroscience of Enlightenment* (2011)

Ready, Romilla and Kate Burton. *Neurolinguistic Programming for Dummies* (2004)

Rinpoche, Wangyal Tenzin. *Healing with Form, Energy and Light* (2002)

Riskowitz, Narina. *Lifting the Veils of Illusions, 7 Steps to Spiritual Enlightenment* (2016)

Roberts, David. *12 Dimensions of Consciousness and Beyond* (2018)

Sagan, Carl. *Pale Blue Dot: a Vision of the Human Future in Space* (1997)

Schwartz, Robert. *Your Soul's Gift* (2012)

Shostak, Seth. http://sethshostak.com (n.d.)

Snowden, Ruth. *Jung: The Key Ideas* (2010)

Sri Swami Satchidananda. *The Yoga Sutras of Patanjali: Commentary on the Raja Yoga Sutras* (2012)

Stein, Diane. *Essential Reiki* (1995)

Stein, Diane. *Essential Reiki Teaching Manual* (2007)

Strassman, Rock. *DMT: The Spirit Molecule: A Doctor's Revolutionary Research into the Biology of Near-Death and Mystical Experiences* (2000)

Talbot, Michael. *The Holographic Universe* (1991)

Thomas, Chris. *The Fool's First Steps: The True Nature of Reality* (1999)

Thomas, Chris. *The Journey Home* (1998)

Thomas, Chris and Diane Baker. *Everything You Always Wanted to Know About Your Body but So Far Nobody's Been Able to Tell You* (1999)

Thompson, Claire. *Mindfulness & the Natural World: Bringing our Awareness Back to the Nature* (2013)

Tolle, Eckhart. *A New Earth* (2005)

Tzu, Lao. *Tao Te Ching* (fourth century BC)

Villoldo, Alberto. *Soul Retrieval* (2005)

Villoldo, Alberto. *The Four Insights* (2007)

Ware, Bronnie. *The Top Five Regrets of the Dying: A Life Transformed by the Dearly Departing* (2012)

Williamson, Marianne. *A Return to Love: Reflections on the Principles of A Course in Miracles* (1992)

The Chopra Centre

www.chopra.com

Heart Math Institute

www.heartmath.org

Contact the Author

Narina Riskowitz
Transformational coach and therapist
Bright Future Now
Email: narina@brightfuturenow.co.uk

www.foundationsofmastery.com

www.liftingtheveilsofillusion.co.uk

www.brightfuturenow.co.uk

About the Author

Narina Riskowitz works as a transformational therapist and soul coach and has developed a series of workshops and meditation courses for personal and spiritual growth. *Foundations of Mastery* further builds on her book, *Lifting the Veils of Illusions, 7 Steps to Spiritual Enlightenment* published in 2016. Since then, she has worked with individuals and groups to take their evolution from self-development to self-mastery. This process of mastery is now captured in this new book as an advanced, yet highly practical, 12-step guide to mastering mind, body and soul.

For more on the author and her work, visit

www.brightfuturenow.co.uk

www.foundationsofmastery.com